COURT IN THE ACT

Humorous Moments from
Australian Courts

COURT
in the ACT

Humorous Moments from Australian Courts

Beverley Tait

Illustrated by
Sean Leahy

The Federation Press
1992

Published in Sydney by

The Federation Press Pty Ltd
PO Box 45, Annandale, NSW, 2038.
3/56-72 John St, Leichhardt, NSW, 2040.
Ph (02) 552 2200; Fax (02) 552 1681.

National Library of Australia cataloguing-in-publication

Tait, Beverley.
Court in the act : humorous moments from Australian courts.

ISBN 1 86287 100 0

1. Trials – Australia – Anecdotes. 2. Trials – Australia – Humor. 3. Courts – Australia – Anecdotes. 4. Courts – Australia – Humor. I. Leahy, Sean II. Title.

347.94075

© Beverley Tait

This publication is copyright. Other than for the purposes of and subject to the conditions prescribed under the Copyright Act, no part of it may in any form or by any means (electronic, mechanical, microcopying, photocopying, recording or otherwise) be reproduced, stored in a retrieval system or transmitted without prior written permission. Enquiries should be addressed to the publishers.

Cartoons by Sean Leahy
Typeset by The Federation Press, Leichhardt, NSW.
Printed and bound by Australian Print Group, Maryborough, Vic.

FOREWORD

It is with great pleasure that I accept the author's invitation to write the foreword for *Court in the Act*. Beverley Tait and I first met in 1987 when I was President of the Human Rights & Equal Opportunity Commission and she was a court reporter recording what became known as the Toomelah inquiry into the sufferings and deprivations of Aboriginal residents of the towns of Toomelah and Boggabilla on the NSW/Queensland border. Sadly, the inquiry arose out of violence in the nearby town of Goondiwindi. While it was a hearing of tremendous poignancy and drama, there were times when the emotional tension of the occasion was relieved by some humorous moments, with everybody sharing in the laughter together.

Court in the Act contains a wonderful collection of these and similar humorous moments that serve to lighten the otherwise serious and formal atmosphere of the courts.

It is a quick and lively mind that can spot the humour and record the absurdity occasioned by misuse of language. Beverley's great sense of good humour and acute appreciation of the faux pas, malapropisms and human foibles which enliven court proceedings will provide the readers of this work with an insight into the lighter side of the law.

This collection of wit is sure to entertain a far wider audience than those individuals from the bar and bench who inadvertently provided the material.

The Hon Justice Marcus Einfeld
Federal Court of Australia

"My shorthand isn't very good."
"I am pleased to hear it, and not at all surprised. Language is too beautiful, too serious, too subtle in its proper form for a sensitive person to easily reduce to scrawls upon a page. Mr Pitman is responsible for more cultural debasement than ever was laid at poor Genghis Khan's door."

Fay Weldon, Little Sisters

This chronicle of our profession's folklore marks the disappearance of penwriters from Australia's courts. It is dedicated to my fellow reporters around Australia who have assisted me in debasing our culture with the heritage of Isaac Pitman. Thank you for your camaraderie – and for the laughter we shared.

CONTENTS

Foreword 5

Introduction 8

Chapter 1
The Judicial Humorist 13

Chapter 2
How the Other Half Works 26

Chapter 3
... And the Reporter Kept on Writing 43

Chapter 4
How the Other Half Loves 64

Chapter 6
Confusion in the Court 100

Chapter 7
The Right Word 113

A Final Submission 128

INTRODUCTION

> Traddles now informed me ... that a perfect and entire command of the mystery of shorthand writing and reading was about equal in difficulty to the mastery of six languages, and that it might perhaps be obtained by dint of perseverance in the course of a few years. I have achieved that savage stenographic mystery. I make a respectable income by it. I wallow in words.
>
> *Charles Dickens,* David Copperfield

When my youngest son, Andrew, was 8 years of age, I attended his school fete. As soon as I arrived, his new teacher drew me aside and said, "I've been so looking forward to meeting you. Tell me – just what is it that you and your husband *do*?".

Intrigued, I told her that my husband managed a financial institution, while I, as a member of the Commonwealth Reporting Service, used high-speed shorthand to provide verbatim transcripts of Commonwealth Courts and inquiries.

"What a let down", she said, disappointed. She explained that, during a class discussion on occupations, Andrew had stood up and announced: "My father does things with other people's money; and I forget the name of what my mother does, but she's one of those fast ladies!".

While court reporting might lack the racy flavour envisaged by that teacher, being a "fast lady" for 16 years has, in fact, been great fun.

The truth of the old cliché that the spectator sees most of the game is nowhere better illustrated than in

INTRODUCTION

the position of the court reporter, who is ensured of a front-row seat in the nation's courtrooms, parliaments, tribunals and special inquiries. From that front-row seat, the reporter faithfully, inconspicuously and impartially records the events which will be tomorrow's headlines.

When the old question, "And what do you do?" was asked, I'd respond, "I'm a court reporter", and the enquirers' eyes would light up. "What a fantastic job that must be!" was invariably the reply.

In their mind's eye, they saw me sitting enthralled on a tension-filled film set while Perry Mason-type lawyers unfolded dramatic plots, Rumpoles entertained the assembly with Wordsworth asides, and Charles Laughton look-alikes produced with a flourish a surprise witness for the prosecution.

The truth is that the vast majority of hours spent in the nation's courtrooms are in long, droning legal argument that produces stifled yawns, lulling the reporter into that strange phenomenon of writing "overdrive" which enables one to write on, faithfully and accurately, while the conscious mind compiles a shopping list or makes plans for the next weekend.

I was once caught out beautifully in the Federal Court before Pincus J, where I had been writing along steadily in "overdrive" without hearing a thing, while my conscious mind planned what food I would take on a forthcoming boating weekend.

Suddenly, like the dreaded interruption of the morning alarm into my dreams, came the judge's voice from behind me: "Would the reporter read back that section of the evidence, please?".

I had heard nothing of the last 15 minutes of evidence, and had no idea what section he was referring to. (I had just reached the chicken and coleslaw for lunch on the second day.) Vaguely flipping through my notes, I hoped I was giving the impression that I knew what I was looking for.

Fortunately, the reporter who was to follow me had been sitting in the chair beside me listening to the evidence. He scanned my notes over my shoulder, pointed to a section of evidence written about 10 minutes before, and whispered, "Read from there".

I did. The judge said, "Thank you", and the hearing proceeded. I had no recollection at all of having heard or written the words I read out.

Because much of real-life court proceedings have this soporific effect, those of us who have been forced to sit through them day by day treasure the sudden flashes of humour and humanity that sparkle occasionally like phosphorous through the dull, turgid sea of legal jargon. In the heavily formal atmosphere of the courtroom, those moments of humour, lancing through the pomposity and pretentiousness, achieve an incongruity that gives them an acute edge.

There are also, of course, many scenes of great sadness and emotional tension, such as the deportation case where the deportee's Australian wife and children sit sobbing behind the bar table; the Criminal Court, where an accused's entire future depends upon the evidence; or the emotionally-draining Family Court.

This chronicle, however, is not about those. It is about the inadvertent moments of levity, the faux pas, the human foibles, and the malapropisms and mis-use of words caused by nervousness and unfamiliarity with legal process, all of which enliven proceedings in our courtrooms.

INTRODUCTION

Unfortunately, some of the best behind-the-scenes-in-the-courtroom stories cannot be recorded, for they lose their pith when the protagonists are not identified. So, mindful of this country's laws regarding libel, and remembering the Oath of Secrecy that I took upon my appointment as a court reporter, I have in most cases refrained from mentioning specific names. There are occasional exceptions, but only where the stories are so well-known that it would be pointless not to name the person involved.

Nevertheless, if any of my learned friends of the bench or bar cares, in private and amongst consenting adults, to recognise himself or herself within these pages, he/she may feel free to do so. I admit nothing: and I reserve my right not to reply, on the ground that it would almost certainly incriminate me.

There is a vast folklore of anecdotes, which are related in court corridors, at office parties, in country motels, in legal chambers – wherever court staff meet and relax. Those recorded here have come to me from Australian, American and English reporters, Judges, Commissioners, associates, and all manner of court attendants and attenders.

Some of the stories have circulated for so long that they have become apocryphal. I discovered, while watching a television episode of "Rumpole of the Bailey", that the court folklore has even longer tentacles than I had imagined. A version of a story I had been told by several Queensland reporters – one of whom named the town, the judge involved, and said he was in the courtroom at the time – was related by Rumpole over a glass of claret in Pommeroy's Wine Bar.

That story was about the alleged rape victim who, confused and blushing, was hesitantly giving her story.

COURT IN THE ACT

Finally, after much embarrassment and side-stepping of the issue, she reached the point in her evidence where she whispered that the man's penis had just entered her vagina. "Right", said the judge heartily, "Let's leave it right there until two o'clock" – and he adjourned for lunch.

Chapter 1

THE JUDICIAL HUMORIST

> And that *Nisi Prius* nuisance, who just now is rather rife,
> The Judicial humorist – I've got *him* on the list!
> They'd none of 'em be missed – they'd none of 'em be missed.

So sang the Lord High Executioner in Gilbert and Sullivan's *The Mikado*, while listing those people whose loss would be a distinct gain to society at large. On the contrary, the humorous offerings which fall from the bench would be greatly missed by reporters. I cite the following cases.

POLICE PROSECUTOR: When the accused was arrested, he said to the arresting officer: "Just you wait. I will be seeing my mate, the Judge".
His Honour: Well, here I am, mate!

IN A CIVIL DAMAGES case, the plaintiff's case was that, because of the trauma he had suffered, he could no longer have normal sexual relations with his wife.

The prosecuting counsel asked how often he did manage to have sex: to which the plaintiff replied, "Infrequently".

As quick as a flash, His Honour asked him, "Is that one word, or two?".

A TOWNSVILLE DISTRICT Court judge was hearing a case of two prisoners charged with wilful and unlawful destruction of three concrete baubles which were originally attached to the parapet on top of a building. The offenders had rolled the baubles over the edge of the building onto the street below.

"Making a eunuch building of it?", asked the judge, ingenuously.

AN ECCENTRIC FEMALE judge in Dade County (United States) is renowned for giving maximum sentences of "up to 1600 years" – and over.

Once, in an unlawful wounding case, she listened intently as the witness described how she had been raped by the victim, then managed to grab a gun and shoot him in the groin.

The judge grinned and leaned over the bench. "Nice shot", she applauded.

A DEFENCE COUNSEL was pleading for a short sentence for his client.
Counsel: My client does have a long criminal history I admit, Your Honour, but since the commission of this particular offence, he has seen the error of his ways, he has found a stable job and intends to stay in honest

employment. He has also met a lovely young girl, and they have become engaged and plan to get married.
His Honour: Well, I hope she believes in long engagements.

ONE PARTICULARLY VAIN 56-year-old judge showed a keen interest when the accused, asked to guess the age of a witness, said, "About the same age as you, I'd say, Your Honour".
Two days later, when that particular witness was sworn in, the judge's first question to him was, "What is your age?".
"42", replied the witness.
The usual petulant judge turned upon the accused a smile of such benign warmth that all in the court were amazed.

BARRISTER: What occasion did you say it was?
Witness: They call it Mother's Day.
Barrister: Why do they call it Mother's Day?
Witness: God knows – ask him.
His Honour: You mean take it on appeal to a higher court?

THE MAN IN THE dock was charged with drunkenness and being disorderly in a public place. He looked at the court clock nervously: "I should be at work at the dry dock by now".
Prosecutor: What do you do at the dry dock?

Accused: Work up a thirst. If you give me another chance, I can go back to work at the dry dock.
Magistrate: Relax. You are in the dry dock now.

―――

COUNSEL: Mr Orderly, call the witness Crutch, please. He is also known as Smith, if he does not answer to Crutch.
His Honour (sotto voce, to the reporter): If my name was Crutch, I'd call myself Smith, too.

―――

VOLUBLE WOMAN WITNESS: Now, look here, Mr Judge, Your Worship, Your Magistrate, Honour – what are you, anyway?
His Honour: Many people have pondered that question, Madam. However, you may for now address me as "Your Honour".

―――

COUNSEL: You did not like your mother-in-law coming to visit you, did you?
Witness: No. May I tell you why?
His Honour: There is no need. That is something we all understand.

―――

HIS HONOUR *(to the jury):* Now, before we begin, I must ask you to banish all bias and pre-conceived knowledge of this case from your minds, if you have any.

―――

JUDGE DUNN OF THE Supreme Court in Queensland would have appreciated this one, although it actually

THE JUDICIAL HUMORIST

occurred before Justice James P Dunne of the Supreme Court in Brooklyn, United States:
Counsel: You are rather anxious to testify, are you not?
Witness: Who, me?
Counsel: Yes, you.
Witness: Why, yes, I am anxious.
Counsel: Why are you anxious?
Witness: Who, me?
Counsel: Yes, you.
Witness: Well, I am anxious to see justice done.
Instantly, Justice Dunne asked, "Who, me?".

INGRATIATING WITNESS: I would like some time to look at this, please, but only if it is at Your Honour's convenience.
Judge (straight-faced): Well, whatever you like. I was actually planning to show it to you here in the courtroom.

QUESTION: You claim you had nothing stronger than a cup of tea?
Answer: No, I am a teetotaller — I don't even drink tea.
His Honour: In that case, you are not even a teetotaller!

WITNESS (brought from prison to give evidence): I'm not bragging or anything, but I want you to know I've got a law degree from LaSalle, and I'm just telling you so that you'll know you're not dealing with a dummy.
His Honour: I'd like you to know I have a law degree from the University of Washington, and you're not dealing with one, either.

ONE QUEENSLAND SUPREME Court judge was a stickler for the hearsay rule. He would admit no evidence of a conversation unless it could be corroborated by another person present at the time.

The accused was giving evidence about his activities on the night in question: "I went over the fence into a yard, when I lost my way. Then I realised it was not the yard I was supposed to be going into, so I hopped another fence and went into the yard beside that. A dog came up to me and started to bark, and I said to the dog ..."

"Stop right there", interrupted the judge. "You cannot say what you said to the dog, witness, unless he is being called to corroborate it."

PROSECUTOR *(in a rape trial, where the alleged victim claimed she had woken up while the man was raping her):* When did you actually wake up?
Witness: While he was raping me.
Prosecutor: Do you mean he had just entered you?
Witness: What do you mean?
Prosecutor: Well, could you estimate for us how far he had entered you before you woke up?
Witness: Oh, yes, I'd say about that long. (She indicated with her hands a distance of about 35 cm.)
His Honour: Well, Madam, I hope you won't drop off to sleep in the witness box, because I certainly could not wake you up.

ONE DAY A SOLICITOR mentioned to her husband, who is a judge, that a client of hers had appeared before him recently, and was scheduled to do so again soon.

THE JUDICIAL HUMORIST

"Then," said the judge to his wife, "you must not, of course, tell me his name."
"Of course not", she replied. "It's just that it was funny when he mentioned you to me, because he said, `I am coming up before your father again soon.'"
"Who is the bastard?", demanded the judge.

WITNESS: I had no vision at all of the road ahead or behind, because I was completely sandwiched between two trucks at the time.
His Honour: An iced Volvo, as it were?

HIS HONOUR: Your wife complains that you wasted your time catching snakes and selling them, instead of working the farm. What do you say to that?
Witness: I did not waste time. I did catch and sell carpet snakes – and I got $50 for one, too.
His Honour: Fifty dollars? It must have been a wall-to-wall carpet snake.

THE PROSECUTOR HAD suggested that a man in the dock be remanded until the following Wednesday, the 11th.
Accused: Could we make it some other day? Wednesday is an unlucky day for me.
His Honour: Very well – we will make it Friday the 13th.

WITNESS (petitioning for divorce on the grounds of cruelty, because of her husband's obsession with sex): He wanted it before breakfast; he wanted it after breakfast; he would come home for lunch and have it before lunch;

then he would want it again after lunch; then in the evenings, as soon as he came home, and after tea again; and then during the night he would wake me up and want it again.
Barrister: What was your husband's health like at the time?
His Honour: Surely that question is rather redundant?

MR JUSTICE MACKEN, addressing the Australian Shorthand Reporters Association at its Seminar on 11 September 1985, said:

> Today the judiciary is expected to be both aloof and wise and yet to keep a common touch so as to encourage litigants to feel relaxed and, hopefully, even truthful in court. The distant and Olympian detachment of the past is not now well received. I can well remember a barrister friend of mine once describing a very aloof judge by saying, "The way Judge X believes in himself is very refreshing in these atheistic days when so many people believe in no God at all".

A NOW-RETIRED FEDERAL Tribunal head, known for his truculence and lack of humour, was not amused to note that whenever a particular reporter in her micro-mini skirt entered or left the courtroom, the barristers at the bar table became distracted from their submissions.

During the luncheon adjournment, she was in the corridor behind the court, checking her makeup in the mirror of her powder-compact.

The judge marched past her, growling, "Before you come back into my courtroom, you had better powder the other cheeks which are also on view!".

THE JUDICIAL HUMORIST

MAGISTRATE *(to reveller on drunkenness charge):* What were you doing in the park?
Accused: Nothing. We were just sitting there under the fig trees.
Magistrate: Well, you should have kept away from the fig trees – they have caused people trouble in the past, you know.

THIS JUDGE WAS quick to pick up a common error, when he was asked that the three prisoners be "re-arranged" (instead of rearraigned).

"Right", said the judge, pointing to the prisoner on the left, "You move to the right end of the dock, and the other two change places with each other."

COURT IN THE ACT

JUDGES ARE NOT the only courtroom humorists. Doctors called to give expert evidence also compete for the laughs – as do some witnesses, inadvertently, through unfamiliarity with medical terminology:
Question: Now, Doctor, you have told us that this man was shot in the street?
Answer: No, I said nothing of the sort. I said he was shot in the lumbar region.

QUESTION: Doctor, how many autopsies have you performed on dead people?
Pathologist: All my autopsies have been on dead people.

DOCTOR: On examination, I found that the man had bilateral peri-orbital and sub-conjunctival haematoma.
Counsel: And did he have two black eyes?
Doctor: Yes, that is what I just said.

HIS HONOUR: Do you have a record of what X-rays were taken at the hospital?
Doctor: I have an X-ray report of chest and sternum.
His Honour: Who are they?
Doctor: What?
His Honour: Do you have difficulty hearing? Who are Chest and Sternum? Are they radiologists?
Doctor: No – your chest and your sternum.
His Honour: Oh.

THE DOCTOR WAS GIVING evidence about his work in the busy casualty department of a large metropolitan hospital:
Question: I suppose you do have some people that suffer trauma, that do not say anything or do anything?
Answer: Occasionally, but they are unconscious.

A NEIGHBOURLY DISAGREEMENT over a fence had developed into an all-in street fight with fence palings and garden tools. Asked whether she had been hurt in the fracas, one witness replied, "No, sort of in between the fracas and the belly button".

JUDGES AND BARRISTERS HAVE somehow developed the idea over the years that reporters have super-human hearing, which enables them to pick up what is inaudible to the normal human ear.

This exchange occurred when a medical expert was mumbling secretively into his hand:
Witness: With regard to the environmental mutagenesis in carcinogenicy, the splenomegali – well, the nitrosamides, shigella, in the case of sodium thiocyanate, o-methylation of guanine ...
His Honour: I can't make out a word of this, Mr ... Can you get your witness to speak up?
Barrister: It is all right, Your Honour. This is being taken down, and Your Honour can read it later in the transcript.

EXPERT TESTIMONY CAN come from an unexpected source. This occurred during a trial for rape, which was alleged to have taken place in the front seat of a Mini Minor. The judge remarked that he did not see how this was logistically possible.

The young associate leaned across and spoke in a whisper to the judge.

His Honour then announced to the court that, contrary to his previous assumption, he now had it on good authority that such a feat could, indeed, be achieved.

———

HIS HONOUR: How long have you practised surgery as a surgeon?
Doctor (sotto voce, to the reporter): Is he for real?

———

IN ANOTHER INCIDENT, the associate's help was not so gratefully received. It was in a probate case involving four brothers, and the presiding judge was hard-of-hearing:
Witness: So then he told me to go to the bugger.
His Honour: Which brother?
Witness: He told me to go to the bugger.
His Honour: There are four brothers. Which brother did he tell you to go to?
Associate (in a loud stage-whisper): Bugger, Your Honour.
His Honour (startled): Mr Associate, I'll speak to you later in my chambers.

———

EVEN THE USUALLY DISCREET and formal court orderlies cannot resist throwing in a line occasionally. In the

course of examining a long series of medical witnesses, a barrister announced, "I now call Dr Stone".
Orderly: No appearance.
Barrister: Then I call the next on the list of witnesses, Dr Smith.
Orderly: No appearance.
Barrister: Then I will ask the Orderly to call whichever doctor on my list is still waiting.
Orderly's Voice (off-stage – in the corridor outside): Is there a doctor in the house?

QUESTION: As a result of the incidents you have described, what can you tell the court about your injuries in relation to your ears?
Answer: I lost my hearing in my left eye.

ON ONE MEMORABLE OCCASION, it was the accused who had the last laugh:
His Honour (in Queensland Supreme Court): You have been found guilty. Have you anything to say before sentence is passed upon you?
Accused: Yes. BEAM ME UP, SCOTTY!!!

Chapter 2

HOW THE OTHER HALF WORKS

> ... the work – the chance to find yourself. Your own reality –
> for yourself, not for others – what no other man can ever
> know. They can only see the mere show, and never can tell
> what it really means.
>
> Marlow (trying to repair the steamboat),
> in Joseph Conrad's Heart of Darkness

The Industrial Courts, Arbitration Commissions and Industrial Relations Commission of Australia are peopled by some colourful and diverting characters, the stalwarts of our industrial relations system. Working in them has given me unparalleled opportunities of sitting at a conference table watching the adroit negotiating skills of Bob Hawke (in his ACTU days); of travelling around the country with such whimsical and boisterous characters as the great raconteur, Arch Bevis Snr (former President of the Transport Workers Union), Wally Curran (Secretary, Victorian Meatworkers Association) and Norm Adsett (former Queensland Secretary of the Storeman and Packers' Union) who once threw this celebrated insult at an opponent: "You are a barnacle on the backside of industrial relations in this state!". The Australian Conciliation and Arbitration Commission (as it was then called) also afforded me the dubious privilege of writing shorthand "on the hoof" in meatworks, foundries, oil plants, fertiliser factories, and while strap-hanging on a bus. I have scribbled my way beside Commissioners and Judges in railway goods-yards, tripping over sleepers and trying to avoid the shunting wagons. At 6.45 am, in a freezing Westerly wind, I wrote with numbed fingers at the gates of a meatworks. I have scratched at my notebook while skidding on fat and scraps on the floor of a noisy Northern Territory boning-room, nudged by huge, bloody carcases moving along the chain beside me.

I have scrawled what looked like pages of barbed wire in a Piper Cub light aeroplane, as it bumped and bobbed across western Queensland, and in a helicopter with Coldham J, as it hovered over an oil rig in Bass Strait.

I have reflected on the good fortune that led me to my own job, as I watched women standing on concrete floors in cold rooms packing meat; a worker in a soft-drinks factory staring for 8 hours a day into a bright screen, searching for impurities in passing bottles; women with wrinkled fingers shelling prawns in humid Darwin; or men labouring in the throat-choking atmosphere of a fertiliser plant.

However, one witness made me realise that, though an occupation might not be to *my* taste, it could have great appeal to someone else. He was a local government plumbing inspector in a north Queensland shire, who gave evidence in a work value case before Commissioner Sel Hastings. It was at the end of a long, hot day and, as we still faced a drive of several hours back to Townsville, Cr Hastings had been trying to "wind him up" for some time.

Undeterred, the plumbing inspector went on and on, obviously enthralled with his topic of sewerage. He expounded at length – as my hand grew more and more tired – on the various types of sewage he had encountered. He waxed lyrical on the finer points of sewage disposal, on the giant rats and frogs that inhabit the sewerage drains, and lingered lovingly over descriptions of the various consistencies of solid and liquid wastes.

Finally, as the clock's hands neared 6 pm, Cr Hastings broke in: "I really must ask you to finish there. I think we have heard enough on this topic".

"I'm so sorry," replied the plumbing inspector, noticing the time at last, "but sewerage is such a fascinating topic, I could talk about it from now until Christmas!"

To each his own. That man would probably have felt an affinity for the union advocate in the Coal Industry Tribunal, who submitted that his members deserved better remuneration because of "the effluent society" we live in.

The same advocate later complained bitterly about the multi-nationals who were, he said, "like a giant octopus, spreading their testicles all over the country!".

I am indebted to all those folk who have given me such fascinating glimpses into their working lives, including the following:

UNION WITNESS: ... down the hill and run across the floor of the dining-room, and you go up to the counter to get your tray, and you keep skidding across the floor and sitting down in the sheep droppings. It's a shit of a way to eat your lunch.

UNION ADVOCATE: Mr Commissioner, I have had prepared a list of our members working at this plant. They are listed under job categories and gradings, and have also been broken down by age and sex.
Commissioner (dryly): Most of us eventually are, are we not?

WITNESS: I didn't want to take on any extra overtime, but the boss kept going on and on about it, so eventually I copulated.

Union Advocate: The vote was put to our members, and it was a unanimous decision: 50/50.

IT OCCASIONALLY HAPPENS that, after a long day of questioning, a lawyer will unconsciously fall into the witness's manner of speaking. This was recorded in a hearing regarding the reinstatement of a security man:
Barrister: And he then told you – what – to get off his case?
Witness: He said, "Get off my fucking case".
Barrister: Did he actually say, "Get off my fucking case?".
Witness: Yes, he did. He said, "Get off my fucking case".
Barrister: And *did* you get off his fucking case?

DURING A CASE INVOLVING members of the Chemical Workers' Union, an advocate was discoursing upon the possible effects of certain substances upon human blood – specifically that of his members – when he coined the word "homogoblin".

When he repeated it several times, it became too much for one of the other advocates present at the bar table. He proceeded to illustrate this new word in a noble drawing, which was then passed, via the reporter's table, to the Commissioner on the bench.

For reasons of delicacy, the drawing is not here reproduced.

Advocate: You did not see what was happening behind your back?

Witness: There was a big commotion going on and a lot of jabber. It's hard to describe – men going mad – going berserk, running around. Some had clothes, some had no clothes. Some had a pair of boots on, and nothing else. It was just like 20 men in a bull ring.
Commissioner: Did you finish your shift that night?
Witness: Are you kidding?

———

A MILL HAND, seeking reinstatement in his old job, explained that he had been unavoidably absent for some time while he served his term on a conviction of rape with violence. He gave his occupation as: "stripper and grinder".

———

THE NEW AUSTRALIAN employee had been accused of making obscene references to the foreman which, in deference to the female reporter, had been written on a piece of paper.

As he waited for the paper to be brought to the bench, the Commissioner asked whether the accused could read English.

"Not too good", was the reply.

The Commissioner looked at the piece of paper. "Well, you are learning fast", he said.

———

ADVOCATE *(speaking of the sewerage plant at Willawong):* I would submit that the Commissioner should be loath to lift the lid on this matter.

———

A UNION REPRESENTATIVE was complaining that the female staff members often refused an instruction to strike. The women were strongly defended by one witness, who stoutly proclaimed: "In the last strike, I can honestly say that every woman staff member went off".
The Commissioner (to general laughter): Perhaps you had better re-phrase that.
Witness: I'm sorry, Mr Commissioner. What I meant was that they all went off to a man.
The Commissioner: That will do. Perhaps it would be wisest if you did not seek to clarify that further.

―――

INDUSTRIAL ADVOCATE: I noticed that Your Honour blanched at the expression, "five and one-half employees".
His Honour: I did blanch at that a little, especially as it is a meatworks matter. I wondered if they had run afoul of the slaughterman.

―――

A PROSTITUTE WAS in the witness box, called to give evidence about a family member's financial dealings. The witness was very vague and made no effort to assist:
Witness: I can't remember any dates because the bloke who was my pimp at the time stabbed me in the head with a screw driver.
Counsel: You say that, as a result of that, you cannot remember anything at all about that?
Witness: No. It was a heavy duty screw driver.
Counsel: Well, can you tell us at which bank you keep your bank accounts?

Witness: I don't trust banks. I keep all my money under the mattress. *Counsel:* But you have given evidence that you have sometimes had large amounts of money.
Witness: Yes, and it's all under the mattress.
Counsel: What – even up to $30,000?
Witness: Look, love, what could be safer? I spend half my life on my back on top of it.

Later, to the great interest of all in court, the questioning went into details as to her daily work schedule, the types of jobs she would engage in, and the kind of men who availed themselves of her services. On the last point, she proclaimed loudly: "Most men go to prostitutes at some time in their lives", then, looking slowly around the room, "Seventy-five per cent of men in this room would have been with a pro".

There were red faces and much innocent gazing at the ceiling from the bench and bar table.

Eventually, she was excused from the witness box, and went to sit in the front row of the public gallery, where she soon became bored. Producing a needle and thread, she sewed up the hem of her micro-mini skirt, twisting it and herself into the most awkward and revealing positions as she worked her way around.

QUESTION: Do you have any friends or relatives in the real estate business?
Answer: Yes, my wife's cousin is a real estate salesman.
Question: What sort of work does he do?
Answer: Pretty sleazy.

WITNESS (in a damages case): When the police arrived, I told them I was not injured, and I would go straight

COURT IN THE ACT

back to work. However, when I later removed my hat, I found that I had a fractured skull.

QUESTION: Can you explain why you were away from work almost every second day during that period?
Witness: I had to go to the chiropractor.
Question: Why were you visiting the chiropractor?
Answer: Well, I was sick in the mornings. I was pregnant, and I was told by someone that it was possibly due to a spinal misalignment.

BARRISTER: Would you identify yourself to these proceedings, please, in relationship to the child?
Witness: Yes, I am his Sixth Grade emotionally disturbed teacher.

And, from another – not surprisingly – out-of-work teacher:
Barrister: Are you employed at the moment?
Witness: I am actually a relief English teacher, but no-one hardly ever very seldom calls me, so I don't get much work.

QUESTION: So you are not working at the moment?
Answer: No. I will be three months' pregnant on 8 November.
Question: Apparently, then, the date of conception was 8 August?
Answer: Yes.
Question: And do you remember what you and your husband were doing on that date?

HIS HONOUR (to juror, wishing to be excused): You say you run a one-man business?
Juror: Yes, Your Honour. It was a two-man business, but my brother is dead just at the moment.

IN A 1986 MATTER before the Federal Court, a Queensland judge endeared himself to the female reporters with this comment:
Barrister: You say you went from being just a housewife with six children, to working 100-110 hours a week in the hotel?
Witness: Yes.
Barrister: Perhaps that had something to do with the nervous exhaustion you developed?
His Honour: Really, that would probably be a reduction in hours, I would think.

IN THE SAME CASE, regarding the itinerants who lived at the back of the hotel:
Barrister: Was it worth keeping those rooms operating?
Witness: They didn't always pay their rent, but they always drank in the bar, patronised the bar. They were always full all the time I was there.
Barrister: What – the rooms, or the tenants?
Witness: Both, I guess.

QUESTION: What was he using to clean the shoes?
Answer: Petroleum jelly.
Question: Petroleum jelly – what is that?

Answer: Vaseline. It is generally used by prostitutes and people like that; but sometimes it is used for guns and patent leather boots.

———

IN THE CANBERRA COURT of Petty Sessions, an Italian witness was being sworn in:
Question: Your name is?
Answer: Guiseppe ...
Question: Your address? *(The address was given.)*
Question: Your occupation? *(The witness did not understand.)*
Question: You are a waiter?
Answer: Ah – nine-a stone five.

———

COUNSEL: Now, I put it to you that on 15 December last you attended your office Christmas party. There you drank six large pots of beer, after which you consumed several Scotches. I then put it to you that you noticed the two girls from the typing pool, Miss A and Miss B, leaving the party, and followed them out of the building. As they waited at the bus stop outside, I put it to you that you approached them and vomited on the footpath. You then asked them to accompany you to your home and tried to force Miss A into a taxi. When she refused, I put it to you that you loudly abused her, and when Miss B intervened, you pushed her away, causing her to fall into the gutter where she struck her head and suffered a severe contusion to the forehead. Now, witness, is what I put to you true or false?
Witness: What was that date again?

———

WITNESS (POINTING): Then he hit me on the right shoulder.
Barrister: But you are pointing to your left shoulder.
Witness: That's right. I am left handed.

CONVICTED DRUG TRAFFICKER *(asked whether he had anything else to say before a deportation order was placed upon him):* How is an honest crim expected to make a living anywhere?

THE DEFENCE COUNSEL was desperately trying to establish that his clients, "massage parlour workers", were in fact employed in a legitimate business.

He had asked them, before they came to court, to bring details of genuine clients who used their services for therapeutic massage only. The women had difficulty thinking of any such case, until one remembered, in the witness box, a client who came in every week to have his fingers massaged to relieve his arthritis.

"Good", said the barrister. "Now, can you remember anything else about him?"

"He was 95, Sir", replied the witness.

ACCUSED *(charged with bigamy):* I left my wife and went out bush droving. I met this woman and started playing around with her. After a time, she said she was pregnant, so we got married. After we were married, she told me she was not going to have a baby, so I said, "Well, we are quits – you are not married, either!".

COURT IN THE ACT

BARRISTER: What is your occupation?
Witness: A Greek.
Barrister: What is your nationality?
His Honour: Why did you ask him that? He just said he is a Greek.
Barrister: I asked him his occupation and he told me his nationality; so I thought if I asked him his nationality, he might tell me his occupation.

WITNESS: People were making some comments to the bar attendant, who happened to be female at the time.

COUNSEL: Is it true or is it false that, on several occasions while you were working as a barman at the hotel, you had sexual intercourse with the manageress while standing in the linen cupboard?
Witness: No.
Counsel: No? Are you saying that you never on any occasion had sexual intercourse with the manageress?
Witness: No.
Counsel: What are you saying, witness? Did you or did you not have intercourse with the hotel manageress on several occasions in the linen cupboard?
Witness: No. Never. It was in the stores cupboard.

A FARMER WHO had objected to his tax assessment was giving evidence before the Taxation Board of Review:
Question: Was your land affected by the 1974 floods?
Answer: No, not at all.
Question: Not at all? That is surprising – I thought all of that area was under about 20 feet of water?

Answer: Oh, yes, it was under water all right, but it wasn't *affected.*

Later, from the same witness:
Question: Do you have an agistment agreement with your neighbour?
Answer: No, he lets my cows go in and eat his grass.

A NORTH QUEENSLAND POLICE Constable was in the witness box:
Constable: I went into the Sergeant's office and told him there was a report of a dead horse lying in Dalrymple Street.
Question: What did he say?
Constable: He said to go and drag it round the corner into Poole Street.
Question: Why did he tell you to do that?
Constable: I think it was because the Sarge couldn't spell "Dalrymple".

QUESTION: Have you had any injuries to your head?
Answer: None fatal.

AN APPLICANT CLAIMED that his health problems were stress related and caused by his work. In rebuttal, it was put that the stress he endured came from his homelife, since he had found out that his wife was working as a prostitute.

The now-separated wife, subpoenaed to give evidence, maintained a defiant air:
Counsel: What would you say, Mrs ... , if I said that your husband had discovered that you were not visiting your

mother or your girlfriends in the evenings, but you were actually in regular work as a prostitute?
Witness: I'd say: prove it.
Counsel: I show you a chemical analysis sheet from X Laboratories, showing an analysis done upon your underpants on 17 May this year, which shows that there were four types of semen identified on them, none of which matched your husband's. What would you say to that, witness?
Witness: I guess I'd say: "Touché!".

IN A BRISBANE COURT, a policeman gave evidence that his legs were being massaged in a parlour where he had gone to seek evidence of illegal practices. He said that suddenly, the masseuse stopped, and said, "Hang on, you've got copper's ankles".

The undercover officer assured her that he was in fact a real estate salesman – but his companion's premonitions proved correct when a police raiding party arrived shortly afterwards.

Questioned later in court, the woman told her lawyer that she could always recognise a policeman's ankles because of their size.

IN ANOTHER HEARING in north Queensland, evidence was being recorded of a policeman who disrobed to get evidence in a massage parlour, and then asked the attendant what he would get for his $100 fee. She told him. The Prosecutor asked him what happened next.

"I sent a message to my Inspector, who was waiting outside", he said.

"And what was that message?"
"Don't send help, sir."

———

IN A TAX CASE before the Federal Court, it became clear what the former owner of a massage parlour really thought of her clients: for tax purposes, she had called her business, "Animals in Distress".

———

ON THE TUESDAY OF a four-day trial, the judge was reading the previous day's transcript, as the cross-examination proceeded. He noticed that a couple of light asides he had made had been recorded in the transcript. "Good grief", he muttered to himself, "They put every bloody thing in this."
   On Wednesday morning, he leafed through Tuesday's transcript. Sure enough, there was his exclamation of the previous day, faithfully recorded.

———

WITNESS *(giving evidence about a robbery in a shoe shop):* And all the shoes were man-made, Your Honour.
His Honour: What – you employ no women at all?

———

COUNSEL: You were doing 10-15 km/h at the time, I suggest?
Police Constable: At the very most, I was doing 5 km/h.
Counsel: What gear were you in?
Police Constable: In my police uniform, of course.

———

WITNESS (a Senior Sergeant of the Victorian Police, commenting on a woman's claim that the accused had wilfully exposed himself): With the advent of the cooler weather, this sort of thing usually drops off.

ONE MAN HAD achieved the ultimate in job satisfaction:
Question: Is your husband happy with his job?
Witness: Oh, yes, he has been unemployed for years.

Chapter 3

... AND THE REPORTER KEPT ON WRITING

> "Who stuffed that white owl?" No one spoke in the shop;
> The barber was busy, and he couldn't stop;
> The customers, waiting their turns, were reading
> The *Daily,* the *Herald,* the *Post,* little heeding
> The young man who blurted out such a blunt question;
> ... And the barber kept on shaving.
> ... Just then, with a wink and a sly normal lurch,
> The owl, very gravely, got down from his perch,
> Walked round, and regarded his fault-finding critic,
> (Who thought he was stuffed) with a glance analytic,
> And then fairly hooted ...
> ... And the barber kept on shaving.
>
> *James T Fields, "The Owl Critic"*

Like that deadpan barber, court reporters become adept at quietly keeping on doing their job while some remarkable and bizarre things occur in courtrooms. "The show must go on", is not a maxim peculiar to actors.

THE *SYDNEY MORNING HERALD* of 2 May 1986 reported that the NSW Parliament had, the previous day and night, conducted a marathon 24-hour sitting.

It quoted the Head of Hansard, Mr Tom Cooper, as saying that he could not remember a longer one in his 28 years of service.

Asked how his reporters had coped, Mr Cooper replied: "They did what is always done – just kept going".

ON THE QUIET, sunny morning of Thursday 14 May 1987, Mr Taniela Veitata was making his maiden speech as an Opposition Member of the Fiji Parliament.

It was being recorded by a dark-haired shorthand reporter named Annie Sue, Fiji-born, of Chinese descent.

Suddenly, Mr Veitata found himself staring into the threatening guns of Lieutenant-Colonel Rabuka's commando squad of 10 masked soldiers, who halted Parliament, kidnapped the Government, and turned Fiji's usually peaceful world upside down.

Undaunted, Annie Sue wrote on, and recorded for posterity the following remarkable verbatim report of what followed the entry of Colonel Rabuka and his men:

Stranger: Sit down, everybody, sit down. This is a takeover. Ladies and gentlemen, this is a military takeover. We apologise for any inconvenience caused. You are requested to stay cool, stay down and listen to what we are going to tell you.

Colonel Rabuka: Please stay calm, ladies and gentlemen. Mr Prime Minister, please lead your team down to the right. Policemen, keep the passage clear. Stay down, remain calm. Mr Prime Minister, Sir, will

you lead your team now. *(The Prime Minister and Government members left the chamber.)*
Colonel Rabuka: *Dou raici koya na turaga ni ovisa sa laka oqori.* [Look out for that inspector; keep him covered.] Sir, could you *(referring to the Opposition side)* lead your team down to your area of assembly. *(The Opposition members left the chamber.)*

Annie Sue concluded her report with a conscientious understatement: "The House adjourned at 10.04 am".

―――――

IN A QUEENSLAND COUNTRY COURT, I watched a reporter write with equanimity while a scraggy chook wandered into the courtroom, stepped delicately across in front of the bar table, and paused to "cluck-cluck" loudly in front of the addressing counsel.

―――――

A QUEENSLAND BARRISTER was noted for his habit of not wearing a shirt beneath his bar jacket during the summer months. As he raised his arms to illustrate a point, reporters would be confronted with his bare, hairy navel – into which, as he pondered a point, he would occasionally twist a contemplative finger.

Only once was he up-staged – by his junior, who listened to the evidence while loudly flossing his teeth with rubber bands.

―――――

A WELL-KNOWN SYDNEY Crown Prosecutor would lean back with a nonchalant air while counsel for the defence was speaking, and rock backwards and forwards in his chair. Every now and then, he would tip too far backwards, and disappear in a flurry of black gown and shoes.

The judge always instructed the Jury: "Take no notice; he's just over again".

... And the reporter kept on writing.

IN THE COURSE OF A TRIAL conducted in an old wooden court house in a dry, central-western town, proceedings were suddenly interrupted when the witness, in mid-testimony, suddenly pointed to the reporter's table and squeaked, "There's a rat under there!".

The colour drained from the female reporter's face, but she valiantly tucked her feet up under her chair and kept writing.

The scene degenerated into pure farce as the bailiff began chasing the rat around the courtroom, and the witness and women in the gallery climbed onto their chairs.

Fortunately (for court process, if not for the rat) the bailiff proved swifter than the poor, bewildered rodent. With a large and heavy boot, he performed a summary execution.

The carcase of the rat was removed and the furore subsided. The defence counsel pointed out that the rat had not been afforded the opportunity of being represented by counsel: nor had it been judged by a jury of its peers.

"Nevertheless," remarked the prosecutor, "it did have a speedy trial."

A little shakily, the reporter merely noted: "Short Adjournment", and went on writing.

ANOTHER UNSCHEDULED SHORT adjournment occurred once on a freezing winter's day in Longreach, when the judge arranged for a heater to be placed behind his chair on the bench. It was an open two-bar radiator. Counsel was well into his opening address, when he noticed wisps of smoke curling up behind the judge.

"Excuse me, Your Honour," he said politely, "but is it possible that your gown is on fire?"

With admirable aplomb, the judge announced a short break, then stood up, flung off his gown, and began stamping on the fire. He was joined by the orderly, and for some seconds they executed a very strange and energetic pas de deux.

The quick-thinking orderly then produced a pair of scissors and trimmed off the burnt section of gown. Court resumed. The reporter went on writing.

COURT REPORTERS ARE OFTEN stopped in the corridor or approached by someone at the reporter's table during an adjournment by someone who says, "I've been watching you. You're incredible. How fast can you write?".

A Sydney reporter was thus approached one afternoon as he was running late for the resumption of a hearing. "You must be able to write about 400 words per minute to do this job", said the bystander.

"That's right, mate", he replied, hurrying into the courtroom.

Throughout that afternoon, the witness talked a blue streak, and the judge several times asked him to slow down for the sake of the reporter.

When this occurred yet again, to the reporter's great embarrassment, the man from the corridor raised his hand in the public gallery and said, "Your Honour, there's no need for you to worry about that man. He told me he can write at 400 words per minute". ... with rapidly reddening neck, the reporter kept on writing.

———

IT ALL BECAME TOO MUCH for one long-retired Sydney reporter. He refused to write with anything but a old-fashioned steel-nibbed pen. When the evidence accelerated, he would splash ink-blots all over himself and the desk, as he frenziedly dipped his pen into a bottle of ink.

Late one afternoon, close to his retirement, the speed of the questions and answers coming at him was so unrelenting that he became completely distracted. Head down, feet planted firmly apart, he had written on and on, splattering himself with black spots as his hand flew in a blur from ink-pot to notebook.

At last he could take no more. Throwing back his chair, he shouted, "This is hell!" and flung his pen at the ceiling, where it became deeply embedded, and remained for many years as a conversation piece.

———

IN SOME OLD-STYLE COURTROOMS, instead of having a separate table in front of the judge, the reporter sits up on the bench alongside the judge. It is not easy to maintain a bland, non-committal air at such times when – as once happened to me – the judge whispers

... AND THE REPORTER KEPT ON WRITING

in one's ear, "If this bloke isn't careful, he's going to hang himself!".

ANOTHER SYDNEY REPORTING friend is still wondering about the logic behind the statement of a judge some years ago, who admonished a rapid-fire speaker: "Slow down, please; my reporter has a speech impediment".

ON ANOTHER SUCH OCCASION, while a reporter sat alongside the judge on the bench, quietly writing, a nervous farmer who was to give evidence came into the courtroom still smoking. This was not noticed for some time until the judge, a particularly ardent non-smoker, slammed his hand on the bench and yelled, "PUT OUT THAT CIGARETTE!!".

The expletive which emanated from the reporter, who rose several feet in the air, was not recorded.

———

A YOUNG BARRISTER WHO regarded himself as dreadfully trendy would sweep up to the court each day in his Aston Martin. He wore the latest in fashion, had a back as stiff as a ramrod, and delivered his submissions in awkwardly pompous, Oxford-accented tones.

He eventually appeared before a wag of an Irish judge, who was popular with reporters for his earthy asides. The judge listened in fascination to the first few sentences of the barrister's submissions, then leaned across the bench to the reporter, and whispered: "I'll bet this bloke never had a spew out the back of a Brisbane tram!".

———

THIS INCIDENT OCCURRED when I was working in London in 1989 although, unfortunately, I was in another courtroom at the time.

A Staffordshire barrister was delivering a serious address when he leaned against the bar table and activated his musical underpants, a Christmas present from his family.

Once started, the musical repertoire had to continue until the end, and the luckless barrister continued his submissions to the accompaniment of Jingle Bells, Tannenbaum, and Rudolph the Red Nosed Reindeer.

... Much cheered, the reporter kept on writing.

———

... AND THE REPORTER KEPT ON WRITING

SOMETIMES REPORTERS DO such a good job of being inconspicuous, that they virtuallly become invisible. Once, a newly-appointed judge was about to conduct his first case in Ballarat. The courtroom was one which had a very high bench. There were 10 steps leading from the body of the courtroom up to the bench, and the reporters had to traverse these as they took over from each other.

The courtroom was packed with the local judiciary and members of the bar, who had appeared to welcome the new judge. After the formal opening ceremony, with its speech of welcome from the President of the local Bar Council, the reporter was relieved by a colleague, and stood up to leave the room.

Crossing behind the judge, he was about to descend the steps from the bench when his foot caught in a hole in the carpet and he found himself suspended in mid-air. He descended the 10 steps without touching them. At the same time, he flung out his arms for balance, and his shorthand notes flew up towards the ceiling.

Landing on one twisted foot at the bottom of the steps, he executed an elegant Nureyev-type leap, meanwhile raising his arm to neatly catch his shorthand notes, and tottered shakily out of the room.

The barrister at the bar droned on. No-one seemed to have noticed.

ANOTHER EXAMPLE of the invisibility of reporters occurred in the old Bankruptcy Court in Melbourne, where an elderly female reporter was sitting up on the bench beside the judge, steadily writing. It was a few years ago, when ponchos were fashionable, and she was wearing one.

The bench was actually a raised dais about 1 metre high, with no back wall to it, and judges and reporters who sat on it were always conscious of the gaping hole behind them.

On this occasion, however, the reporter became so engrossed in getting down the increasingly rapid questions and answers that, as she bent lower over her notes, she pushed her chair backwards and over the edge.

There was a sudden confusion of woollen tassels, black shoes and white petticoat as she disappeared.

It took her some time to extricate herself and her pen from the poncho, but eventually she managed it, smoothed down her clothes, lifted the chair back onto the dais and climbed back herself.

The questions and answers were continuing as if nothing had happened. The reporter took a deep breath, noted, "Off the Record", and went on writing.

———

WITH THE AUSTRALIAN Broadcasting Tribunal in a Queensland provincial city, during the hearing of an application of a grant of a licence for a community radio station, the reporter wrote poker-faced while the witness explained that the Hospital Hour was sponsored by the local undertaker.

———

A BRISBANE REPORTER managed to keep writing once as the judge, rocking thoughtfully backwards and forwards on his chair as he listened to the cross-examination, flipped himself over backwards.

From his position, the reporter missed the view of those at the bar table, who were treated to the judge's impression of "Wot, no chocolates?" as first his hair, then his eyes, followed by his nose, appeared slowly back up above the bench.

ON ANOTHER OCCASION, the same reporter was sitting up on the bench beside a different judge, when His Honour leaned across towards him to make a sotto voce comment.

To his horror, the judge just kept coming. The leg broke from the judicial chair as he shifted his weight, and he landed head-first in the reporter's lap.

DURING A QUARTER SESSIONS trial in rural New South Wales, a man was charged with malicious injury and causing actual bodily harm.

The history of the case was that the accused, a gentleman of Southern European origin, returned to his home to find his wife and his friend in an act of adultery.

So irate did the husband become, that a wild struggle ensued and, during that struggle, by brute force and without the use of sharp instruments, the left testicle of the adulterer was torn from his scrotum.

During the trial which followed, the Crown tendered the left testicle, which was displayed in a glass container. The container and contents were marked as an exhibit, and placed on the edge of the reporter's table. The reporters did their best to write with averted eyes.

COURT IN THE ACT

At the conclusion of the case, the husband was acquitted and discharged, and the judge ordered: "The exhibit may now be returned to its rightful owner".

WHILE DISTRICT COURT sittings were being held in the Court House in the main street of Bowen, north Queensland, the Gem of the Coral Coast Festival was in full swing in the street outside.

It became increasingly difficult to hear over the sound of a brass band which seemed to be playing on the footpath directly outside the courtroom window.

Eventually, the judge interrupted the barrister who was submitting: "Just a minute, Mr ... Would you care to have an adjournment until this finishes, or will you sing your address?".
Barrister: Your Honour, I think we had better proceed. We have a lot to get through today.
His Honour: Very well. I am finding it impossible to hear you, but it is being taken down by the reporter, so I can read it in the transcript later.

The reporter, who was possessed of no more super hearing than the others present, somehow kept on writing.

THIS STORY (reprinted from the *Milwaukee Journal*) illustrates the very special team spirit and comradeship with which reporters sustain each other when the going gets tough:

Delegates at a Conservative Party Conference in Blackpool, England, were puzzled why the fast speakers were getting more applause. Then one noticed that off-duty shorthand writers were touching

... AND THE REPORTER KEPT ON WRITING

off waves of clapping and foot-stamping, in order to give their working colleagues a chance to catch up.

IN THE ADMINISTRATIVE Appeals Tribunal, an applicant gave evidence that he could not comfortably wear his glass eye all day, and that this prevented his gaining employment in his field, which involved dealing with the public.

His barrister asked him to remove the cosmetic lens to show the bench just how grim the gaping socket looked.

After careful discussion, the three members of the bench ruled that the removal of the eye would not be necessary.

... The reporter resumed writing with her eyes open.

DERMOT NOLAN, Vice President of the Hamilton (Ontario) Law Association, addressing a conference of court reporters, said:

> Court reporters have the most expressive eyes in the Universe, eyes that cry out wordlessly but unmistakeably such things as: "All right! Enough already!". Or, "Are you out of your mind?". Or, "Right on!". Or, "Are we ever going to get out of here?". Or, more frequently, "You really blew that one, didn't you, pal?".

ANOTHER LAWYER ONCE referred to us as: "the unblinking sphinxes". Remaining unblinking can be a masterpiece of self-control while listening to exchanges like the following:

COURT IN THE ACT

A barrister was quietly cross-examining the witness, when suddenly the questions took a new and sharper tack: "I suggest to you that you were offered $2000 to throw this case".

The witness looked at the judge and made no reply. The barrister repeated the question, again getting no response.

Finally, the judge said to the witness, who kept staring at him, "Can you answer that question, please, witness?".

"Oh," said the witness, "did he mean me? I'm sorry, Your Honour – I thought he was talking to you."

———

IN A TRIAL IN western Queensland, a girl complained of having been raped. The complainant was in the witness box:
Defence Counsel: Before he had intercourse with you, did you notice his penis?
Witness: Yes.
Defence Counsel: In what condition was it?
Witness: What do you mean?
Defence Counsel: Well, was it doing anything?
Witness: Doing anything?
Question: Well, was it pointing any particular way?
Witness: Oh, I see – yes, it was pointing towards Dirranbandi *(a town in northwest Queensland).*

———

IN HIS BOOK, *How To Write 250 Words Per Minute In Pitman's Shorthand,* Maurice Kligman tells the story of an elderly lady who had been subpoenaed to court to testify as eye-witness in a damages case.

She talked increasingly faster and faster, panting as if she could not afford to take the time to stop and draw breath. At one time, Kligman looked up at her and saw that she was staring fixedly at him.

Eventually, the judge asked her to slow down. "I just cannot keep up with you, Madam", he said.

"I'm sorry, Your Honour," she replied, "I am doing my best, but I just can't keep up with *him*" – pointing to the sweating, exhausted reporter.

PROSECUTOR: How would you describe your drinking habits?
Witness: I'm only a sometimes drinker.
Prosecutor: What do you mean by: "a sometimes drinker"?
Witness: Whenever I've got the money.

IN A CASE in which a will was contested, the following extract from the will was read out in court:

> To my wife AB, residence unknown, I give the sum of one shilling tram fare to some place unknown, to drown herself. To CB I give nothing – he is not my son; XY is his father – after my death. To my son EF, I leave nothing under my will. He is my son; he was not born a bastard, but he grew up one.

IN ANOTHER WESTERN Queensland case, this time a claim under workers' compensation:
Witness: I was kicked in the back by a dead kangaroo out at St George.
Counsel: How could a dead kangaroo kick you?
Witness: Well, he wasn't dead then, but he soon was.

Prosecutor: You were recorded by the police radar as doing 110 km/h in a 60 km/h zone.
Witness: That's right.
Prosecutor: Was there any reason for your travelling so fast in such heavy rain?
Witness: Well, my windshield wipers had broken, and I had to drive that fast to blow the water off the windshield so that I could see where I was going.

SOLICITOR: Do you know how much money your husband usually carries in his pockets?
Wife (to Magistrate): Do I have to answer that?
Solicitor (for husband): No, you need not incriminate yourself.

THE ALLEGED VICTIM in a rape trial had just finished describing all the dreadful details:
Barrister: What did you do then?
Witness: I remember picking up my hat. It was all crushed up. I said to him, "Look at my hat – and I paid $7.50 for that!".

QUESTION: Was there any plea bargaining?
Witness: Well, it was not really free bargaining – I had to pay a lot of money to get off.

HIS HONOUR *(to man convicted of embezzling):* How on earth could you steal like that from people who trust you?

Embezzler: Well, Your Honour, it's a great deal easier than stealing from people who do not trust you.

WITNESS: As soon as I woke up that morning, I knew it was going to be one of those days when everything goes wrong.
Counsel: Why do you say that?
Witness: Because I woke up with an awful headache; and the next thing was my wife said she was feeling amorous.

QUESTION: My question is, do you suffer from any specifically diagnosed medical condition like Alzheimer's disease or anything that would specifically contribute to the hampering of your memory?
Answer: Not that I can remember.

THE COURT: You are charged with drunkenness, using obscene language in a public place, and abusing a police officer. How do you plead?
Accused: I plead guilty, with a very strong recommendation for mercy.
The Court: On what grounds?
Accused: On the grounds that I am Irish.

POLICE PROSECUTOR: When he was arrested for being drunk and disorderly, all he could say was, "Will I get my grog back?".

Magistrate: Well, did he?
Police Prosecutor: Actually, no.

―――――

BARRISTER: Do you remember the night of 16 April?
Witness: I certainly do. I remember it very well.
Barrister: Well, tell us what happened on that night.
Witness: Nothing.
Barrister: What do you mean, nothing? You have just told us you remember it very well.
Witness: Yes, I remember it very well because that was the night nothing happened.

―――――

LOSING THE CLOAK of invisibility can be nerve-wracking for the reporter. A charge of robbery with violence, where a broken milk bottle had been used as the weapon, was being heard in Brisbane. In the old Supreme Court building, the dock was so high that, when the accused sat down, he could not be seen.

The eye-witness, an elderly man, was being examined in chief. "Can you see the accused in court now?" asked the prosecutor. "Just point to him and identify him for us."

The witness looked at the judge and knew it could not be him; he looked at the men in robes at the bar table and knew it could not be them. The only other person he could see was the reporter. "That looks a bit like him", he said.

The prosecutor was only momentarily taken aback. "Come down out of the witness box into the body of the court, where you have a better view of everyone", he suggested.

... AND THE REPORTER KEPT ON WRITING

The witness complied. He looked around at everyone he could see, and again pointed an accusing finger at the reporter.

Eventually, to loud and strenuous objection from the defence, the prosecutor asked the accused to stand up in the dock, and said, pointing directly at him, "Look at that man over there, witness. What about him?".

At last the witness saw the accused. "Ah, yes, now that *is* him!"

The judge leaned across the bench to the reporter and whispered, "Nearly got you that time!".

―――

ON RARE OCCASIONS the reporter (like the spectator at the Geebung Polo Club, whose "leg was broken – just from merely looking on") has been wounded in action. One Queensland Supreme Court reporter was quietly writing one day as an excitable Southern European plaintiff gave evidence of the mental trauma he had suffered as the result of an accident.

Under cross-examination, the plaintiff became very heated, offered to take on the defence counsel, and started to rip off his coat.

There was a desk calendar on the witness stand and, as he flung off his coat, the desk calendar flew across the room and struck the reporter in the face, breaking his glasses and inflicting a deep cut to his mouth.

With his left hand holding a handkerchief to his bleeding lip, the reporter stolidly and quietly carried on writing. He transcribed the day's work, holding the paper up to the light to see through the blood which had spattered on his notes, before finally visiting a doctor to have his wound stitched at 9 pm that evening.

———

ANOTHER WITNESS, describing a drunken brawl between the defendant and the complainant, was asked to explain how he had wrestled the knife from the defendant.

"I rushed up to him bent over like this", he said, lunging at the reporter's table, and proceeded to provide a graphic demonstration by placing the reporter in a headlock and bending his writing arm up behind his back.

———

I KNOW OF ONLY one occasion when reporters themselves chose to drop their cloak of invisibility.

It was over the issue of whether reporters should bow when entering or leaving a courtroom, a requirement which varies from tribunal to tribunal. Many judges these days feel that, as reporters are an integral part of the court staff who come and go every 15 minutes or so, the practice is unnecessarily distracting: others like to adhere to the old tradition.

In one particular tribunal where bowing was not usually required, a newly-appointed judge with a tender ego complained to the principal reporter that reporters were not showing him sufficient respect by genuflecting as they came into his court.

When this fault was brought to their attention, the team of female reporters assigned to that particular court for the week took remedial action.

For five days the judge was thoroughly distracted every 15 minutes by the sight – behind the backs of all

... AND THE REPORTER KEPT ON WRITING

but himself and his delighted associate – of an entering or leaving reporter, wearing the lowest décolletage she could find in her wardrobe, deferring to the judge in a deep bow.

At the end of the week, the judge asked his associate to tell the reporters that bowing could be dispensed with.

(Ve may be invisible, but ve haf our vays!)

Chapter 4

HOW THE OTHER HALF LOVES

> Had I the heavens' embroidered cloths,
> Enwrought with golden and silver light,
> The blue and the dim and the dark cloths
> Of night and light and the half-light,
> I would spread the cloths under your feet:
> But I, being poor, have only my dreams;
> I have spread my dreams under your feet;
> Tread softly because you tread on my dreams.
>
> *WB Yeats*

Every weekday, the romantic hopes and dreams of thousands of Australians are trodden underfoot in the Family Court of Australia.

Speaking on the occasion of his retirement from the Family Court bench in August 1990, Lambert J said:

> This court disappoints or delights more of the nation's population than any other court. Its judgments affect not only the immediate parties and their children, but reach out to touch their relatives and neighbours and friends, their kin and all who love them.

The Family Court is most likely to be the only court that an individual will face in a lifetime, and the decisions made there affect the protagonists at the emotional level – the very core of their being. As the repercussions of those decisions ripple out through the extended families, they eventually have a profound effect on society at large.

In the Family Court, the reporter becomes a sometimes embarrassed silent listener, privy to the parade of hurts, infidelities, inconsistencies, lies and malice woven into the day-to-day fabric of a less than perfect marriage.

The shortcomings of a spouse may be accepted with wry affection for many years in a happy marriage; but, if that marriage begins to disintegrate, they take on an exaggerated importance. I have silently written as a man raged about his wife's sloppy housekeeping and failure to care properly for his clothes – keeping my eyes downcast, lest he see through the innocent air of the reporter, who had dashed out of the house that morning leaving the bed unmade, and a husband muttering imprecations as he tried to do up yet another buttonless shirt-cuff.

There is often great sadness in the Family Court . One is always aware of the anxious eyes of the petitioner and respondent at the bar table; the apprehensive children at home, whose side is told by the court counsellor, and whose plight is epitomised by the 14-year-old boy who sobs in the corridor outside.

Because of this intense emotional involvement, the air in Family Court can be charged with an almost palpable tension, which places a great amount of pressure on all present. The dash of levity, which relieves the sombre recital of heart-rending pain or accusations of incest, can be particularly welcome; and the stress which surrounds those occasional flashes of humour gives them an added piquancy.

One of the most important things a reporter must learn is to keep a straight face while people fight over custody of a dog; agree to monthly access to their mutual collection of paintings; or even, as in one memorable case, argue as to who should retain possession of the gold toilet-roll holder.

I have remained deadpan as a witness told how the placenta from his wife's home birth, buried in the garden in accordance with their spiritual beliefs, had been dug up by the neighbour's dog and dropped on the kitchen floor. I have not turned a hair as a female witness stated that she was really Marilyn Munro, but had been kidnapped as a child by her father and made to dye her hair black. She described herself as a modern Cinderella.

I have written with equanimity while a husband explained that he could no longer sleep with his wife, because during intercourse she emitted an intergalactic ray that made his teeth tingle for days afterwards.

Despite our expressionless court faces, however, there is much off-beat and diverting riposte which is later shared and savoured in the reporters' rooms:

QUESTION: You say your domestic problems started in the kitchen?
Wife: Yes. When we were first married, if I burnt the cakes, he used to just give me a big hug and a kiss – but now he swears and throws them out the window.

―――

DIVORCE APPLICANT: We separated two years ago, and for the whole of that time, I have been celebrant.

―――

QUESTION: And what was the highlight of your daughter's nine-year-old birthday party?
Wife: Her father's arrival home from the pub with five drunken mates and a live pig in a tutu.

WIFE: He said he had had enough of the dog sleeping on our bed, and it was not right for dogs and humans to sleep together. Then he went out and bought a kennel and put it up in the back yard.
Question: How did you react to that?
Wife: I said, "Fine. I hope you will be very happy in your kennel".

QUESTION: Did you commit adultery with the respondent on this occasion?
Answer: No, not on this occasion, nor any other occasion, nor with any other woman in Brisbane – except my wife, of course.

APPLICANT: My current address is not really ideal, but I have every expectation of being able to provide suitable accommodation for the children soon.
His Honour: What is your current address?
Applicant: Her Majesty's Prison.

QUESTION: What is the current state of your marriage?
Divorce Applicant (an Italian lady): It'sa very good, very good.
Question: Very good? But I thought you had been separated for over two years?

Applicant: That'sa right; two years I haven't seen him – it'sa very good.

QUESTION: What was the first thing your husband said to you when he woke up that morning?
Wife: He said, "Where am I, Cathy?".
Question: And why did that upset you?
Wife: My name is Susan.

BECAUSE THE APPLICANT had made a claim for Social Security payments, the advocate was attempting to establish domicile of his wife and children:
Question: Your wife had been living apart form you in Papua New Guinea for four years, then. When she came down to Australia last year for Christmas, what were your intentions?
Answer: You mean honourable or dishonourable? Well, I had not seen her for a long time, so ...
The Tribunal: Not *those* kinds of intentions, Mr J ...

QUESTION: Did you object to having a large family?
Wife: Well, I told him he might fancy he looked like Clifton Webb, but he could forget that "Cheaper by the Dozen" routine.

HUSBAND *(explaining why he had married his wife):* I had reached the stage in my life where I thought I might as well settle down and make a home. Also, my business was doing well, and she was a book-keeper, so I

thought it would be handy to have her do the books for me.
Barrister: Any other reason?
Husband: My parents thought she would make a good wife for me.
Barrister: Any other reason?
Husband: She was a good cook, too.
Barrister: No other reason?
Husband: Well, yes, she was pregnant.

———

IN LONDON in 1989, I took testimony from a woman who found a novel way to get back at her husband and destroy his desire to spend time with another woman – she laced his food with laxative, which gave him severe and consistent diarrhoea for four months.

Every morning, she crushed Senokot into her husband's coffee and cereals. Then she watched as he spent the rest of the day dashing to the bathroom.

Her campaign of hate – she had spent two years waiting for a divorce – landed her in court, where she was charged with: "administering Senokot with intent to annoy". She admitted the offence and was placed on a one-year bond.

———

QUESTION: Your husband has been keen on gardening for years?
Wife: Well, he said he liked to be close to nature – but I think he just liked to be close to the bottle of rum he kept in the garage.

———

COURT IN THE ACT

ALTHOUGH IT MAY NOT be perfect, the Family Court Act is a vast improvement on its predecessor, the Matrimonial Causes Act, which inflicted the most tortuous and torturous proceedings upon those who sought relief under it. Though fault is no longer an issue, the question of the parties' moral attitudes does become relevant when it comes to the question of custody of the children of the marriage.

So the subject of sexual intercourse does still rear its titillating head at times in the Family Court. As stand-up comics have long known, sex can be a very funny subject.

―――

IN A CUSTODY CASE on Queensland's Sunshine Coast, the wife's sister went into the witness box to corroborate the applicant's claim that her husband was profligate:
Witness (speaking of her brother-in-law): I was down in the patch helping him to pick pineapples, when he came up behind me and grabbed me, and threw me down in the plants and had sex with me.
His Honour: In the middle of the pineapple plants?
Witness: Yes; he was always very keen on me, Your Honour.
His Honour (sotto voce): He must have been. He must have had a very tough hide, too.

―――

THIS WIFE WAS petitioning for divorce and custody. Under cross-examination, she had admitted that she and her husband (a professional couple) had been regularly involved in "swingers" parties where wife-swapping was the norm.

She agreed quite readily with her husband's statement that she and her girlfriend had on occasion provided the star turn for these evenings, by performing Lesbian acts on the lounge-room carpet.
Counsel: Your husband had no complaint about that?
Witness: No. He liked it.
Counsel: So what was it that finally brought your relationship with your husband to a close?
Witness: I came home one day and found him in a homosexual encounter with a chap from his office.
Counsel: And did you not like that?
Witness: Well, no – I mean, a woman has to maintain certain standards in the home, doesn't she?

———

COUNSEL: Was it your husband's practice to knock you about?
Wife: He never needed any practice. He was very good at it.

———

BARRISTER: You say your husband can't stand women?
Wife: Well, I can only speak for myself.

———

QUESTION: Did your husband have any particular hobby to occupy his time?
Wife: My word – it used to occupy his time until 10 o'clock every night, when the pubs closed.

———

QUESTION: If you did not waken when your husband came home that night, how did you know he had come home inebriated?

Wife: Well, apart from the fact that the bedroom smelt like a brewery, I found both bottles of milk broken at the bottom of the front steps when I got up next morning.

QUESTION: Your husband says you never cooked him any meals?
Wife: That is a lie. I cooked him better meals than he would get anywhere else – just look at the fat pig!

OPPOSING COUNSEL: Surely there was nothing to stop you taking your wife to your club socials occasionally?
Husband: You have not been to our club socials.

QUESTION: What started the argument that night?
Wife: I reminded him that it was our wedding anniversary.
Question: And what did he say to that?
Wife: He said, "Don't bring that up while I'm eating".

QUESTION (*to wife of musician*): But that was your husband's profession, to go out playing at night. Why did you object to that?
Wife: I did not object to his going out to play. I objected to his going out to play *up*.

QUESTION: When and where were you married?
Husband: I can tell you when and where, but don't ask me why. I must have been out of my brain.

QUESTION: What did your husband say when you told him you were leaving him?
Wife: He said that was the best thing he had heard come out of my mouth in 30 years.

WIFE: This woman friend of my husband came to see me. She told me that if I had any insurances, I had better look out, because my husband would put poison in my coffee.
Question: Do you drink coffee?
Wife: It depends on who is making it.

HUSBAND: I was only ever interested in my wife's happiness.
Opposing Counsel: But you have had private detectives checking up on her?
Husband: That's right. I wanted to know why she was looking so happy.

DURING ANOTHER FAMILY COURT circuit in the central west of New South Wales, the wife claimed that her husband resorted to all sorts of dreadful perversions, so terrible that she could not name them.

The most she could bring herself to do was to hand up to the court, by way of an exhibit, a bag containing the "evidence" which she said would prove her husband's depravity.

Naturally, the two reporters took the opportunity over dinner that night to ask the judge what the bag contained. He confessed that he was mystified: while the bag did contain one appliance whose purpose was obvious, the remainder of the items comprised such vile items as a notebook and pen, a hand cake-mixer, an alarm clock, a tape-measure, a can of sweet corn and a baby's rattle.

While we never did establish to what exact use the items were put, it certainly provided some lively speculation over dinner that night in the local Chinese Restaurant!

———

QUESTION: According to your husband, you always gave his friends a very frigid reception when he brought them home.
Wife: They did not need it. They were always stoned cold drunk before they arrived.

———

WIFE (speaking of her husband's frequent fishing trips): They always took a carton of rum with them.
Question: Why was that?
Wife: He told me it was in case of shipwreck.
Question: So if they managed to avoid being shipwrecked, they would bring it back intact?
Wife: Never – and they never brought any fish, either!

———

QUESTION: So you smashed six plates of your good dinner set, throwing them at your husband?
Wife: That's right.
Question: You were very angry with him, then?
Wife: No, not *very* – I have often thrown lots more than that.

QUESTION: You say that in the last seven years, your husband never made an affectionate gesture towards you?
Wife: That's right.
Question: He has given evidence about the time at the Exhibition, when he put his arms around your waist.
Wife: Big deal. He crushed three ribs, and I had to go to the doctor.

THESE dreadful indictments could only be heard in the Family Court:

- She was the sort of woman who always took her sewing-machine along when we went on camping trips.
- My husband was so strong that he used to snap his nail-file in half with one hand.
- He was so boring that – well, even when he was young, his brother told me he was the kind of kid that would have run away from the circus to join an orphanage.
- She only married me because the rates on her mother's house were due.

QUESTION: What else did you have to complain about, so far as her house-keeping was concerned?
Husband: Well, she would make a giant-sized stew for tea. Then we would have it on toast for breakfast next morning. Then she would put it in my crib for lunch. Then I would come home from work that night, and we would have the same bloody stew warmed up for tea.

That would go for days until the whole thing was finished.
Question: Did you ever make any objection to this lack of variety in the cuisine?
Husband: Why bother? She couldn't even make a decent bloody stew — but I figured the stew you knew was better than the meat pie you didn't.

QUESTION: I put it to you that your husband never laid a hand on you?
Wife: That's right — he kicked me.

QUESTION: What did you object to about your wife's swimsuit?
Husband: She would have been just as well covered wearing ear-rings.

QUESTION: Your husband is fond of his fishing club outings?
Wife: He was.
Question: Was?
Wife: Yes, the club has disbanded now.
Question: What happened to it?
Wife: It closed down when we decided to form a women's auxiliary.

QUESTION: I suggest to you that your wife did not speak to you in a threatening manner at all. To the contrary, I suggest that, when your wife asked you for her purse back, she spoke in a perfectly reasonable manner?

Husband: I suppose she did. It was what she had in her hand that worried me.
Question: And what was that?
Husband: A lump of three-by-two.

QUESTION: You say your husband always managed to turn the blame round onto you?
Wife: That's right.
Question: Go with telling us what happened that night when your husband arrived back at 3 am.
Wife: Well, as he staggered down the hall, I called out, "Is that you, Joe?" and he said, "Yes, why – who else were you expecting?".

QUESTION: Did your husband have breakfast before he left for work that day?
Wife: He had what he calls breakfast.
Question: What was that?
Wife: A double brandy.

QUESTION: Was your sex life satisfactory?
Wife: Oh, yes, Your Honour, very satisfactory. He worked so hard he was always too tired to trouble me.

IN A PARTICULARLY SQUALID custody case, it had been admitted that the husband had involved his children in many base acts, including forcing them to watch his home videos of their mother in the act of sexual intercourse with himself and other men.

The videos were admitted as exhibits and shown in court, but the gentlemanly judge suggested – to the reporters' chagrin – that they take a short break while they were shown, lest they be embarrassed.

When he came to deliver his decision in the case, the judge, a man with a great sympathy for abused children, asked the father to stand. His Honour pulled no punches in telling the father just what he thought of him. As a father, said the judge, the man was utterly contemptible. His depraved actions had caused irreversible trauma to the emotions of his children that would cause them life-long anguish, and would very likely render them incapable of ever conducting a normal, loving relationship with a person of the opposite sex.

He saw no reason why the husband should ever be allowed to spend unsupervised time with his children again. The tension in the court was almost tangible. The judge's harangue lasted over 45 minutes, as the man stood impassively in front of him.

Finally, the judge paused to draw breath. "Now," he said, "have you anything to say for yourself before I give my final orders?"

"Yes", replied the man instantly, "When can I get my movies back?"

―――

WITNESS: I say to my husband, "I would really like to get dressed up and go out", and all he wants to do is to undress and relax. I don't know where you go from there.

―――

BARRISTER: So you left the party and went down underneath the house, and you found your husband with this other woman?
Wife: That's right. They were in a compromising situation.
Barrister: What were they doing? Did he have his arms around her?
Wife: Well, not right around her – she is too fat for that.

QUESTION: Would you describe him as a heavy drinker?
Wife: Certainly. He must weigh about 18 stone.

HEAVY DRINKER

QUESTION: You say your husband never ever arrived home early?
Wife: That's right.
Question: I put it to you that he *did* arrive home early on the night of your birthday.
Wife: I'll say – *very* early – 3 am!

———

QUESTION: You are telling me that your wife spent $11,000 a year in feeding the family?
Husband: That is right.
Question: Come, come. How could that be possible?
Husband: Well, we like nice wines with our meals.

———

QUESTION: Did you scream or complain when he was attempting to force you to have sex?
Witness: I certainly did. I said, "Be careful, or you will ruin my pantihose".

———

HIS HONOUR (to divorce petitioners): Well, I don't know. Why should I give you two a divorce? If I do, you'll only walk out of here and marry again and make another two people unhappy. Then, in a couple of years, I'll have to re-cycle the lot of you.

———

A PROPORTION OF PEOPLE who appear before the Australian Family Law Court complain about what they regard as its anomalies and inequities. Perhaps they would feel less ill-used if they considered the predicament of the divorce petitioners of yesteryear, who had to resort to Parliament. The following historic instruction relates to the English Divorce by Private Act.

At the instance of Lord Chancellor Loughborough in 1798, Parliament established a regular practice as to the circumstances in which it would grant a private Act dissolving a particular marriage. The nature of that practice is perhaps best summarised by quoting the words of Maule J in passing sentence on one Hall in 1845:

> Prisoner, you have been convicted of the grave crime of bigamy. The evidence is clear that your wife left you and your children to live in adultery with another man, and that you then intermarried with another woman, your wife being still alive. You say that this prosecution is an instrument of extortion on the part of the adulterer.
>
> Be it so; yet you had no right to take the law into your own hands. I will tell you what you ought to have done; and, if you say you did not know, I must tell you that the law conclusively presumes that you did.
>
> You ought to have instructed your attorney to bring an action against the seducer of your wife for criminal conversation. That would have cost you about one hundred pounds.
>
> When you had recovered (though not necessarily actually obtained) substantial damages against him, you should have instructed your proctor to sue in the ecclesiastical courts for a divorce a mensa et thoro. That would have cost you two hundred or three hundred pounds more.
>
> When you had obtained a divorce a mensa et thoro, you should have appeared by counsel before the House of Lords in order to obtain a private Act of Parliament for a divorce a vinculo matrimonii which would have rendered you free and legally competent to marry the person whom you have taken on yourself to marry with no such sanction.
>
> The bill might possibly have been opposed in all its stages in both Houses of Parliament, and

altogether you would have had to spend about one thousand to twelve hundred pounds.

You will probably tell me that you never had a thousand farthings of your own in the world, but, prisoner, that makes no difference. Sitting here as an English judge, it is my duty to tell you that this is not a country in which there is one law for the rich, and other for the poor.

THE LAST WORD on Family Court proceedings should come from the petitioner who made the following perfectly logical response:
Question: What was the feature of your marriage which made you finally decide to end it?
Petitioner: My wife.

Chapter 5

MALAPROPISMS, SOLECISMS & ORS

> There are naive people around who regard philologists as dull, forgetting that the rogue-god Mercury presides over language.
>
> *Anthony Burgess,* Homage to Qwert Yuiop

As Humpty Dumpty said to Lewis Carroll's wondering Alice, "When I use a word, it means just what I choose it to mean – neither more nor less". Because people often have their own highly original version of what a word means – or because they sometimes simply mishear, or do not wish to admit their unfamiliarity with a word, some very funny malapropisms, solecisms, puns, Spoonerisms and other "howlers" have found their way into our court transcripts. Some of them are here recorded:

BARRISTER (in workers' compensation case, to applicant claiming traumatic neurasthenia): What were your emotions like?
Applicant: Quite regular – twice a day.

AN AGED, WEALTHY MAN was petitioning for divorce. He alleged that his young wife had been caught in flagrante delicto with younger men during the course of the marriage. The wife counter-claimed that, on the contrary, it was her husband who had been involved with several younger women.

The judge recalled the petitioner, a very deaf man, and repeated to him the wife's allegations of his misconduct. He then asked, "What do you say to that?".

The petitioner replied in a very loud, indignant voice, "Your Honour, it is a complete and utter fornication!".

———

QUESTION: Can I have bail in my own recognition?
His Honour: But who is going to recognise it?

———

QUESTION: How do you plead?
Answer: Lousy, thank you.

———

A DISTRICT COURT JUDGE is remembered for an inadvertent pun he made in his days at the bar, when summing up his submissions. He was applying for bail on behalf of a chap charged with stealing horses.

His grounds for the bail application were that the accused kept stables, the income from which supported the family and, if bail was refused, the horses would not be properly cared for, the business would lapse, his family would suffer, etc, etc.

"He and his wife work together on a daily basis to maintain the horses," he concluded. "It is in fact a stable relationship."

IN A QUEENSLAND SUPREME COURT case, the judge surprised the Crown Prosecutor by angrily demanding that he re-phrase what seemed to be a perfectly reasonable request to the witness.

Later, upon perusing the transcript, the judge realised his error, and delivered a retraction in court the next morning.

The offensive question had been: "Well, perhaps, during the course of my cross-examination, you could drop the showmanship and just answer the questions, please".

The sheepish judge confessed that, for the word "showmanship", he had heard, "shame and shit".

The Crown Prosecutor accepted the judge's apology.

BARRISTER: Why did you not apply for the invalid pension?
Witness: I tried that, but I could not get it. You have to be 85% decapitated. [incapacitated]

BARRISTER: I take it that, before this accident happened, you lived with your sister and brother-in-law for about six months?
Witness: Yes.
Barrister: You got to know him quite well?
Witness: Yes.

Barrister: So you saw him in interaction with your sister, and I believe they had one child?
Witness: Well, I didn't see the actual interaction, but they did have one child, yes.

IN A FEDERAL COURT HEARING, I watched a new young barrister explaining the details of a previous order. His nervousness made him tongue-tied, and in the course of some confusion about whether the order had been handed down by Judge Spender or Judge Pincus, he eventually attributed it to "Judge Sphincter".

AN ARBITRATION COMMISSIONER'S clerk treasures a transcript which showed the Commissioner, upon resuming after a break to consider his decision, as saying: "Gentlemen, I have had ample time to give due consideration to this matter since we adjourned on 18 March, 1879 ..."

Perhaps he was just a slow thinker!

A WITNESS IN THE Queensland Supreme Court once complained that a transcript had reported him as saying that he and his wife "urinated in the bath". What he *had* said was that they were "united in the faith".

(Pitman writers will recognise the similarity of the outlines.)

WITNESS: And then he pushed me, and I fell straight into the ovulating fan.

WITNESS: It was a great shock to me when the doctor told me I was suffering from a venerable disease.

QUESTION: Is there anything you can offer by way of extenuating circumstances for your driving behaviour on this particular day?
Answer: Well, I was under heavy seduction at the time.

NERVOUS Young Barrister: I appear for the honour, Your Wife.
His Honour: It's about time somebody did.

WITNESS: And then, finally, after nearly a year on the futility drugs, I became pregnant.

APPLICANT (in Administrative Appeals Tribunal hearing): The doctor said I was suffering from insipid hypertension.
His Honour: I think you mean "incipient" – unless it was just in a very weak form?

IN ANOTHER AAT hearing, a belligerent elderly gentleman, upon being asked for the second time whether the hospital he had attended was a

Repatriation hospital, exclaimed: "Of course it is a Repat hospital — I told you before I am a veterinarian".

———

HUSBAND *(explaining why he no longer wished to accede to his wife's divorce application):* I was away working a lot of the time in that last year and, as Your Honour would know, abstinence does make the heart grow fonder.

———

QUESTION *(in Family Court):* Did you tell your solicitor that your husband had offered you indignities?
Answer: He never offered me nothing. He just said I could take the fridge and the washing machine.

———

BARRISTER *(to witness in Family Court):* During the course of your marriage, which one of you did most of the wanking?
Witness (astonished): I beg your pardon?
His Honour: I think you had better try that question again, Mr G ...
Barrister: I'm sorry, Your Honour. I meant the banking.

———

IN A SOPORIFIC TAXATION Board of Review matter, a Barrister once inadvertently made everyone in court suddenly sit up and take notice:

MALAPROPISMS, SOLECISMS & ORS

Barrister: I now move on to my next point, where it seems that the Commissioner of Taxation has a sexual problem.
The Tribunal: He may well have, Mr C ... , but what does that have to do with us?
Barrister: Oops – what did I say? I'm so sorry. I meant that he has a sectional problem.

A LAWYER ONCE REPORTED on his surprise when he read in a transcript that he was reputed to have said, "Your Honour, I feel like a twice-spermed bride". [twice-spurned]

ONE COUNSEL HAD ANNOUNCED that the judge could not look at a certain document referred to in the case. The opposing counsel was of a different view, and stated: "His Honour can sew a veil himself". [so avail himself]

PEN WRITERS IN AUSTRALIA traditionally transcribed their verbatim notes by either (a) reading them face-to-face to court typists; or (b) reading them onto cassette tapes, which then went to a typing pool for processing.

Occasionally, mis-hearings and typing errors have produced transcribed material which is an improvement on the original. My all-time favourites are probably:

> The transcript which had a barrister saying, "I will now move on to the frigging sore point". [the Briggenshaw point]

Or:

"How did you manage to get the notary nude?" [the note renewed]

Or:

Barrister: I now call my next witness, Mr John Wanker, who is the car salesman in question. [Walker]

IN AN ARBITRATION COMMISSION hearing, there was great significance in the fact that a brown-and-white striped shirt was seen lying on the back seat of a car.

Unfortunately, when recording this exhibit in the transcript, the typist omitted the letter "r" in "shirt".

BARRISTER: There is something which needs clarifying in the previous transcript. Did you say he was a Jekyll and Hyde character?
Witness: No way. I said he was a gentleman of high character.

THIS MISTYPE, as it turned out, was prophetic:
Barrister (resuming after luncheon adjournment): If it please Your Honour, I will now continue with my losing submissions. [closing]

A NEW ELEMENT altogether was introduced into a Federal Court case when, "Has he been set aside?" was transcribed as, "Has he been circumcised?".

A MIFFED QUEENS COUNSEL complained to the Reporting Service that the previous day's transcript had recorded the judge as saying to him, "Thank you for your submissions, Mr ... ; they were of infinitesimal value".

He claimed that what the judge had actually said was, "They were of inestimable value".

THE WITNESS HAD BEEN expounding on his knowledge of Existentialism and the works of Albert Camus. The transcript then showed him as saying: "One of my favourites is *Mrs Syphilis*". [*The Myth of Sisyphus*]

QUESTION: Are you absolutely sure about that last answer, witness?
Witness: Your Honour, I can put my hand on the Bible, and look any man in the eye, and say that is what I saw, exactly as it happened – because, Your Honour, I am a believer in absolute voracity.

IN AN AIRLINE STAFF case in the AIRC, there was discussion about the flight attendants' duties with regard to stacking the pantries on board the aircraft. One witness was recorded as saying: "There is not enough room for everything that has to go into the hostesses' panties".

———

A MAN WHO HAD EARLIER stated that he was completely reformed from a life of crime, was later depicted in a transcript as saying that he carried "a sworn-off shotgun".

———

ADVOCATE (in arbitration hearing): Mr Commissioner, we can never reach any consensus on this matter, if the union representative will not stay within the armpit of the award. [ambit]

———

A NEW TYPIST, unsure of the spelling of a company mentioned in evidence, was discovered searching the plumbers' listings in the telephone book for: "The Erstwhile Plumbing Company".

———

AN ELOQUENT COUNSEL, who proclaimed in a murder case: "Justice demands that the defendants be held accountable for her inch-by-inch death, until a merciful God finally gave her peace", was quite deflated when he read in the transcript that he had said: " ... until a merciful God finally gave herpes".

———

ANOTHER EMINENT COUNSEL in Canberra protested that he had been transcribed as saying in his address: "There he sits, like a parrot on a perch", when he had actually said, "like a paragon of virtue".

———

THE OMISSION OF a simple apostrophe once made a world of difference to an employer's evidence. He was reported as saying: "If I do not like you and your behind, I do not have to continue to employ you". [you're]

———

ANOTHER TYPIST OBVIOUSLY made her own snap judgment in a case. Instead of typing, "The witness may now be excused", she substituted: "The witness may now be executed".

———

A LEADING MELBOURNE QC complained, during a Federal Court hearing, that the previous day's transcript had quoted him as saying that the judge had castrated him.
"I think it should be made clear," he said, "that I was not castrated – merely castigated."

———

COMMISSIONER PAULINE GRIFFIN of the Australian Industrial Relations Commission was once embarrassed to read in a transcript that she had asked a most able advocate whether he had now finished his: "substandard submission". [substantive]

COURT IN THE ACT

FROM A TRANSCRIPT TAKEN on arbitration inspections, after inspecting men at work on a building site:
The Commissioner: Well, we will just put that down on the record, because we have a reporter on the pot here. [on the spot]

A BARRISTER ONCE phoned a reporter friend to ask, "Who is Judy Carter?".

"I have no idea", said the reporter, "Why?"

"Well," replied the Barrister, "I have been credited with raising her."

It seems that a typist had transcribed the Latin phrase *res judicata* as "raise Judy Carter".

JUDGE *(correcting, in court, the previous day's transcript):* The transcript reads: "The fence was just high enough for me to wee over". I am sure the witness said it was just high enough for him to *see* over.

IN AN INDUSTRIES ASSISTANCE Commission transcript, the Dairy Farmers Association appeared as "The Fairy Farmers Association"; and an Arbitration Court heading page once announced a dispute between a union and "The Bastard Butchers Association". [Master Butchers Association]

OTHER TYPING ERRORS or mis-hearings which have caused mirth between the reporters and typists are:

- This matter was set down before the senior puny judge. [puisne]
- ... and they began serving dinner just as we flew over the Great Australian Bite.
- She was always pouring over cookbooks, but hardly ever came up with anything edible.
- (From an arbitration hearing): The reason why we have such a high turnover of staff is because we are so frustrated; the company keeps us constantly under-stuffed.
- She was wearing a vaginal white dress.
- He was so tired and thin that he looked quite emancipated.
- The last time I actually saw the diary, it was in the drawer of the Chip and Dale table in the hall.
- I have always been a keen student of nature, particularly flowering native fauna.
- It is an experience largely unknown to the Rankin file. [the rank and file]
- The food was absolutely indelible.
- It was fired by jet-compulsion.
- The air was full of flying orgasms.
- I'm sorry, but I do not find it easy to speak pubicly.
- Soon after he was born, his mother died with purple fever. [puerperal]
- In that respect, we would be looking at an entirely different end of the spectre.
- It is alleged that defect itself stems from a poorly braised emission system part.

COURT IN THE ACT

- Witness, would you describe his penis as placid? [flaccid]
- We were trained in the use of the odd light. [theodolite]
- Well, I saw Gray and my wife lying on the bed. They were evidently talking, and they were in the mood. [in the nude]
- It seems as if you are trying to hasten me into a judgment, and all of you are rushing like lemons towards it. [lemmings]
- Your Honour, this is a crazy judicial matter. [quasi-judicial]
- These matters are really just supposed, are they not? [juxtaposed]
- Your Honour, he was so angry, he was absolutely incest.
- Pursuant to Your Honour's erection, I now seek leave to ... [direction]
- He would come marching into the bedroom every night, demanding his martial rights.
- Then I saw the police coming down the road in a carpet roll. [a car patrol]
- This is the absolute crutch of the matter ...
- He gave me a book, and he said it was a token of his affliction.
- She spun around and kicked me right in the abominable cavity.
- The dermatitis was of Apache nature. [a patchy nature]
- I did not want to cause any more conflict, but he wanted to know when we were getting the

- dogs and pigs, when the cow was going to have a calf and when the mayor was going to have the foal.
- They were members of the bras section of the orchestra. (Female trombone players?)
- The problem of youth in Asia is one of the most difficult moral questions we face today. [euthanasia]
- She carries on as if she is as pure as the drivelling snow.
- The large crane has been released, but the wenches are still being held by officers of the Customs Department. [winches]
- I had to go to hospital to get my aviaries removed.
- There was definite evidence of seamen in her vagina.
- The doctor told me I had sick-as-hell anaemia.- [sickle cell]
- *Bankruptcy Judge:* I order that the estate be sequestrated, with cost$s to be taxed.
- This is a crude jurisdiction, Your Honour. [accrued jurisdiction]
- I am a poof reader.
- The matter was heard by Sir Lionel Bowel.
- The Australian Meat and Liverstock Commission.
- I said I refused to get out of the house until they got an agistment order against me.

A NSW BARRISTER was left scratching his head over the following mystifying statement ascribed to him: "I refer now to the activating 88". [The Act of 1888]

IN *THE LOVED ONE*, his satire on the American way of death, Evelyn Waugh introduced us to the droll mortician who used a novel method to lighten the day of his lady love, the cosmetician. On the face of the occasional corpse that was destined to pass along the assembly line to her, he would fashion a beatific smile.

In like manner, cassette-tapes of transcription which passed between myself and my friend in the typing section, Bev Durrant, sometimes bore private, wry comments on the happenings recorded thereon. In return, completed transcript would sometimes reappear on my desk with one of her delightfully apt and clever limericks attached.

Because they made comment on the people involved, they cannot here be repeated. On one occasion, however, I wrote to Bev from Sydney, where I was working on Frank Costigan's Painters and Dockers Royal Commission, recording chilling evidence about people being fitted with concrete boots and thrown into the harbour.

Her reply – in verse form – came to me from Darwin, where she was typing the evidence at the Lindy and Michael Chamberlain murder trial. In view of the events which have since transpired in that much-publicised case, the verses she sent me at that time have proved eerily prophetic:

MALAPROPISMS, SOLECISMS & ORS

The words now on everyone's lips
'Aint painters and dockers of ships.
He has entered, by jingo,
That phantom dog, dingo,
And all other news he outstrips.

The media's blazoned "AZARIA",
Stressed black trackers' search of the area
Through thryptomene roots
– forget concrete boots –
And herbaceous parietaria.

It beats that old painter and docker
With his victims in Davy Jones' locker.
The Press now has claws,
And dread bloodstained paws,
With which to incite us to mock her.

The scientists put forth their theses,
Foetal blood and electrophoreses;
They've got down to taws
With carnassial jaws,
And teeth and saliva and faeces.

In the evidence of odontology
And the field of forensic biology,
It is plain on its face
That this is a case
Of a bunyip – or parapsychology?

There are mystical old bora rings
To be found there around Maggie Springs.
Pitjantjatjaras, they say,
Are steeped every day
In the lore of unspeakable things.

You may tremble with fear and humility,
But what passeth beyond credibility
Is that *something* was there
Near a wild dingo's lair
And the Wailbiris' cave of fertility.

The evidence tends to bewilder
Was it dingo or Lindy who killed her?
In the ether are hosts
Of Uluru's ghosts,
And the wind whispers "Waltzing Matilda".

Beverley Durrant

Chapter 6

CONFUSION IN THE COURT

> Where I am not understood, it shall be concluded that something very useful and profound is couched underneath.
>
> *Jonathan Swift*

It is not the function of court reporters to assess the lucidity of what they hear. They simply record it. However, there are occasions when they are left shaking their heads and wondering what on earth the speaker meant.

Sometimes a curious muse takes hold of jurists and causes them to ask some very strange questions. On other occasions, the confusion can be caused by the nervousness of an intimidated witness.

Question: Just try to speak slowly and clearly, and tell what happened to the judge.
Answer: Why – what happened to the judge?

―――

BARRISTER: How long is it since you and your wife separated?
Witness: Two-and-a-half years.

CONFUSION IN THE COURT

Barrister: And in that time, have you cohabited at all?
Witness: Only once or twice on the phone.

———

QUESTION: How old are you?
Answer: Twenty.
Question: How far did you go in school?
Answer: Just a couple of blocks down from where I live.

———

BARRISTER: At any period of time after you lost consciousness or do not remember what happened, did you see the car change direction or speed?

———

ADVOCATE IN ARBITRATION COURT: ... (vi) of this clause, Mr Commissioner, is one that escapes Mr D ... and myself. I have checked application, s 6 Industrial Arbitration Act 1940 as amended, and it is just non-existent, and when you do find it, it doesn't make sense in any case, but it always has been.
The Commissioner: That is it broadly, in a nutshell.

———

BARRISTER: Did you in fact sleep with him?
Witness: I can honestly say on oath that I did not sleep a wink with him.

———

QUESTION: Were you acquainted with the deceased?
Answer: Yes.
Question: Before or after he died?

———

QUESTION: When you say you don't remember, how are you saying that?
Answer: I am saying that from memory.

QUESTION: How was your first marriage terminated?
Answer: By death.
Question: And by whose death was it terminated?

THIS CAREFUL INSTRUCTION was given during examination-in-chief:
Counsel: Now, Witness, we do not want you to tell us anything you do not know of your own personal knowledge – not what someone told you, or what you think, or what someone may have told you, but only what you actually know of your own personal knowledge. So, bearing that in mind, can you answer this question: Are you a married man?

BARRISTER: So that if anybody was hitting anybody during that time that you did not see anybody hitting anybody, I assume that nobody could have hit anybody very many times?

QUESTION: Would you say you are irresponsible?
Answer: Not really.
Question: How many times have you committed suicide?
Answer: Six times.

CONFUSION IN THE COURT

QUESTION: You say it is Miss Jones. I take it, then, that you are unmarried?
Answer: Yes, twice.

POLICE WITNESS: He came into the traffic counter and complained that the battery had been removed from under the bonnet of his car.
Answer: What did you do next?
Police Witness: I asked him whether he was sure it had been there when he left the farm to come into town.

QUESTION: In the business arrangements to do with the hobby farm, was your husband the prime mover?
Answer: No, we didn't even have a pick-up truck.

IN ANOTHER CASE, the Barrister was pointing to an erratum in the previous day's transcript. "It refers here to a 'head jog', Your Honour", he said. "I am sure Your Honour is familiar with the term used. It should be a 'head job'."

"Yes," said the judge, "but in another transcript I saw it appear as a 'hedgehog'."

"Perhaps we have some innocent reporters, Your Honour", said the Barrister.

WITNESS: The night before cohabitation ceased, he choked me to death. We only had sex one more time after that. Then he told me to get up and go.

POLICE WITNESS: In other words, he certainly did not state to me he was currently unconscious; nor did he state to me he was not — so I do not know whether he was conscious or not.

―――

HIS HONOUR: Give the court your full name, please.
Witness: Philamena Isolteveine Smith.
Reporter: Would you spell that, please?
Witness: S-M-I-T-H.

―――

DISTRACTED COUNSEL: And you are the husband of the defendant — I am sorry; I mean you are the husband of the plaintiff?
Woman In Witness Box: Actually, I am the wife.

―――

NERVOUS PROSPECTIVE JUROR: Judge, I would like to be excused from the jury, because my wife is about to become pregnant.
Counsel: Your Honour, he does not mean his wife is about to become pregnant; he means she is about to deliver.
His Honour: He is excused. In either event, he should be present.

―――

QUESTION TO A POLICE WITNESS: Now, officer, on the occasion in question, where were you located, if anywhere?

―――

CONFUSION IN THE COURT

COUNSEL: Witness, please look at this photograph, which has been marked "Exhibit 12". Now, do you recognise yourself in that photograph?
Witness: Yes, that is me there on the right.
Counsel: And do you recall whether you were present when that picture was taken?
Witness: I cannot remember.

———

QUESTION: Where was your mother born?
Answer: Dover, England.
Question: Do you remember when?
Answer: 1911.
Question: Could you tell us the date?
Answer: No, I don't think I was born then.

———

SOMETIMES THE LAWYERS get themselves tangled up in a private confusion:
Mr Smith: Now, if Your Honour pleases, Mr Brown knows that is an improper comment, and I object to it.
Mr Brown: I object to what he thinks I know. He does not have any idea what I know. I know what he does not know.
Mr Smith: No, I am afraid Mr Brown does not know what I do not know.
Mr Brown: I know what you do not know.
His Honour: I am afraid you both have lost me. Could the reporter read that exchange back to me, please?

———

QUESTION: At the first time you saw the accused, had you ever seen him prior to that time?

———

COUNSEL: If you have a feeling, a sense, or a memory of something that might have been, but you need to qualify it, you can go ahead and tell us – but do not speculate at all.

———

PROSECUTOR: Did you interview them separately or alone at that stage?
Witness: Sorry – could I have that again?

———

WITNESS: She was suffering from a fractured tibia in her right arm.

———

QUESTION: By comparison with the list of duties that you have made up yourself of what you do here, and your duties in your previous job, is there any close similarity between the two?
Answer: They are very much alike.
Question: So there is a close similarity?
Answer: No, not similarity, but they are alike.
Question: Well, in what way are they alike?
Answer: Not really alike – just that they are similar to each other.
Question: I think we will move on to the next point.

———

QUESTION: You say he was cruel to you. What did he do to you?
Answer: He hit me, and then he bit me.
Question: You say he hit you. What did he hit you with?

Answer: His fist.
Question: And what did he bite you with?

AS IF SUCH SCRAMBLING of the English language is not enough, the reporter has another problem to cope with. As Lord Casey (quoted in Bill Hornadge's *The Great Australian Slanguage*) said:

> Many Australians are mumblers ... being a little deaf, I am frequently at a loss as to what they are talking about.
>
> Australians are great exponents of what John Davenport labelled, in a 1949 New Yorker article, "Slurvian". Reporters have to cope with the kind of poorly articulated, slurred speech that produces "guvment"; "lays and gemmen"; the storm that brought "flashes of lining in the mill of the nigh"; "I called a pleaseman"; and the witness who, recently returned from his European holiday, says he has "just been Nittley".

IN A COURT TRANSCRIPT, there is no room for explanations or stage directions. Any commentary is kept to a minimum. Thus, when a small, shifty-eyed witness wipes his forehead yet again with his screwed-up handkerchief, rises from his chair and trips over the edge of the witness box in his eagerness to scuttle nervously out of the courtroom, that whole potential vignette appears in transcript simply as: "Witness excused". The record speaks for itself.

Occasionally, though the record may be a true account of what was actually said, it speaks strangely. Reporters have to write, helpless, as various types of misconceptions in communication take place. They have to grit their teeth and resist the urge to correct

COURT IN THE ACT

the record, even though it seems at times to be a record of misunderstandings.

Sarcasm is a notorious confuser of the record. Once, in the Family Court, a witness was responding to allegations made by his wife.

Obviously amazed and disgusted that she could level such unfounded charges against him, he sat back in the witness box shaking his head in wonderment, and made such derisive replies as, "Oh, sure"; "Of course, I beat her all the time"; "Yes, yes, that's just the kind of thing I would do" – when it was clear that he meant the exact opposite of the words I was writing down.

It irked me to transcribe that section without an explanatory note, for I knew the opposing barrister would make hay with those affirmatives in the transcript when the case came back on appeal.

CONFUSION IN THE COURT

QUESTION: And what was your uncle's name?
Answer: Wright.
Question: Right – his name?
Answer: Wright.
Question: Are you saying r-i-g-h-t?
Answer: W-r-i-g-h-t.
Question: Oh, Wright.
Answer: Right.

WITNESS: Then I saw a person running towards me.
Counsel: Can you describe the person to us?
Witness: No, it was too fast. The only thing I can be sure of was that it was a person with a thick, dark beard.
Counsel: Could you tell whether it was a male or female person?

Barrister: Do you know how he was when he was alone?
Witness: I cannot remember ever being with him when he was alone.

WITNESS (describing other possible eye-witnesses to a murder committed in an hotel): At the most, there would have been no more than 2 or 3 at the least.

A WITNESS IN THE Arbitration Commission took care to clarify a point: "If he is assistant, he is not assistant to the leading modeller; the leading modeller is the assistant to the assistant. I think the assistant modeller is a modeller. I do not know where the assistant comes in. If he is assistant, he is not assistant to the leading modeller assistant. The leading modeller is the assistant to the assistant. He is the one that is giving the tuition".

———

QUESTION: Did you see the plaintiff fall from the roof?
Answer: Yes.
Question: And did you observe in which direction she fell?
Answer: Downwards.

———

QUESTION: What is your name?
Answer: John Smith.
Question: And what is your marital status?
Answer: Fair.

———

WITNESS: There were five of them there.
Question: And were they male or female?
Witness: Both.
Question: Both sexes were represented, or each person there was male and female?
Witness: How do you mean?
Question: Do you know how many males and how many females?
Witness: It was two of each.
Question: But you said there were five?
Witness: The last one was anybody's guess.

———

COURT ORDERLIES AND BAILIFFS have been known to make their own contribution to courtroom confusion. One Supreme Court bailiff was renowned for dropping off to sleep after lunch each day.

On one occasion, the defence had some submissions to make in the absence of the jury, who were ensconced temporarily in the jury-room. "You had better find me some authorities on that point," said the judge, "and I will hear you further in the morning."

Someone woke up the bailiff, who adjourned the court, and everyone present went home at 3 pm.

At 8.30 pm, one the court cleaners was startled to see a very worried and hungry jury foreman peering tentatively around the door. The bailiff had forgotten to let them out.

———

ANOTHER SUPREME COURT bailiff, also prone to nodding off, was dozing peacefully one day while a detective in the witness box, who had been given permission to read from his notes, read what he had noted down on the night in question.

Looking up at the gallery, the judge noticed a spectator in the front row reading a *People* magazine. "Mr Bailiff", he hissed loudly, "Tell that man to put that book away."

Awakening suddenly, the bailiff drew himself up straight, marched forcefully over to the witness box, slammed his fist on the rail and demanded in a loud, formal voice: "PUT THAT BOOK AWAY, SIR!".

———

STAYING AWAKE seems to be the most difficult facet of a bailiff's job. Another bailiff went off into dreamland in what was known in Brisbane as the "toy court", a small, narrow room with a large cedar door and frosted windows. He was sitting in a corner beside the bench, where he could not be seen by the judge.

At 4.30 pm, court rose and the associate closed the court. Everyone left and went home, completely overlooking the bailiff, who slept on.

Some hours later, he awoke to pitch darkness, and stumbled around the room crying, "I can't see! I'm blind! I'm blind!" until he was rescued by a cleaner.

THE HIGHEST COMMENDATION for contribution to courtroom confusion, however, must go to the judge who made the following ruling: "It is, except to the extent that it is not".

> Words are like leaves; and where they most abound,
> Much fruit of sense beneath is rarely found.
> *Pope, "Essay on Criticism"*

Chapter 7

THE RIGHT WORD

> Words, words!
> What useless tools
> Man has created.
> What worth a device
> That fails at time
> Of greatest need?
>
> Inamorato, incomparable,
> Ineffable, indescribable:
> The only words that touch
> The meanings sought
> Are those which prove
> Words fail their purpose.
>
> *M Hall*

If, as the Bard told us, a rose by any other name would smell as sweet, it seems logical that the sexual act by any other name would feel as good.

However, it seems this is not so. Many polite citizens of our society object to the use of the more graphic four-letter words. One particular old Saxon word – though common now in film and on stage – is still regarded as unacceptable in newspapers and raises a storm of protest whenever it is heard on our airwaves.

COURT IN THE ACT

One Christmas week in the mid-80s, while Santa Claus jingled his bells in the street outside, I and two other reporters spent an edifying day reporting a hearing of the Australian Broadcasting Tribunal as it engaged in an exercise in semantics relating to *that* word.

Listeners to an FM radio station had objected to the playing of a song whose repeated lyric was, "Too Drunk to Fuck", and the day's earnest debate was whether the lines, "Too Drunk to Make Love", or perhaps, "Too Drunk to Have Intercourse", would have been more acceptable – though no-one seemed to care about their failure to scan.

In Australia, as in England, the test for obscenity is whether the literature in question tends to "deprave or corrupt".

In the United States, however, some very important judgments on obscene literature were given by Mr Justice Frankfurter of the US Supreme Court. Author and ex-barrister John Mortimer (speaking at an ABC literary lunch in Brisbane in 1990) said: "The definition of obscenity was that which was likely to give Mr Justice Frankfurter an erection".

"In the history of American law," Mortimer continued, "it was noticed that, as the years went on, the learned gentleman's definition of obscenity became considerably more lax."

Though some members of our society earnestly endeavour to defuse the shock effect of four-letter words by overusing them until they become meaningless, the community at large still finds certain words obscene and offensive. However, what is obscene to one individual is quite acceptable to another; and a person who in certain company peppers his conversation with obscenities may, in other circumstances, affect to deplore them.

In the same way that people are loath to listen on the radio to words which they might use quite readily in the ordinary course of their daily lives, so, too, are they loath to use those particular words in the heavily formal atmosphere of the courtroom. The most macho labourer can become incredibly coy about uttering in those hallowed halls words which would liberally garnish his everyday conversation with his mates.

ONE SUCH WITNESS was a burly meatworker who gave evidence in the Family Court that, before his ex-wife brought his small son to visit him on access weekends, she made a suggestion to the boy which was so filthy and embarrassing that he simply could not bring himself to say it in open court.

"I'm afraid," said the judge, "that you cannot make vague allegations like that. If I am to accept that as evidence, I need to know the actual words she used."

Looking sideways at me, the witness said, "Your Honour, I'm afraid I just can't repeat it in front of a lady".

The judge looked around the courtroom. "Lady?" he asked, in surprise, then – seeing me sitting below the bench – "Don't worry about that", he smiled, "That's just a reporter".

Still the witness maintained his coy stance, until eventually he was persuaded to write the dreadful words on a piece of paper, which was handed up to the judge.

Naturally, I took the opportunity during the morning-tea break to ask the judge's associate what had been written. It transpired that the vile instruction to his son, which the husky, tattooed meatworker had been quite unable to voice in my presence, was: "When you go to Daddy's house, do a poopy on the floor!".

AT AN ARMY PLATOON party, a stripper had been engaged to provide the entertainment.

As the girl performed, one soldier became overcome with excitement and kept grabbing at her breasts. A Corporal gave him the order to desist, which the soldier ignored. Seeing his duty, the Corporal struck the soldier and dragged him outside.

Thwarted, the soldier pulled out a knife and tried to stop the Corporal, inflicting a wound. A court martial was called to consider what punishment should be meted out.

Throughout the court martial, it was interesting to note that the various soldiers called to give evidence became overwhelmed with shyness in the presence of the female reporter, and resorted to embarrassed references to the stripper's "knockers", "boobs", and even "tits" – anything at all but the perfectly respectable "breasts" which, strangely, they were unable to articulate.

ONE IRASCIBLE OLD QUEENSLAND District Court judge had long given up sticking to the niceties of language. In a trial in a coastal provincial city, the prosecutor had been trying to drag out of the witness how much he and his friends had had to drink on the night in question:

THE RIGHT WORD

Prosecutor: How much did you take there?
Witness: One dozen stubbies.
Prosecutor: How many did you drink?
Witness: Maybe seven or eight stubbies each.
Prosecutor: Were you affected by alcohol?
Witness: I would not say that.
Prosecutor: Not by seven or eight stubbies?
Witness: Well, should I be?
Prosecutor: How many does it take before you become affected?
Witness: How do you mean?
His Honour (all this ducking and weaving had finally became too much for the judge, who fixed a baleful eye on the witness and demanded): Look, all the prosecutor is asking you is whether you were half-pissed or not!

THE FORMAL LANGUAGE OF a courtroom can cause a block in communication with an unsophisticated witness. In some cases, the unashamed used of a colloquialism can provide the key to understanding.

A Queensland Supreme Court judge has been oft-quoted for his earthy resolution of this problem:

An unlawful carnal knowledge trial was being heard in the far-west. The alleged victim was a terrified, 15-year-old Aboriginal girl. Thoroughly intimidated by the odd-looking men in black gowns and wigs, all she could do was tremble in fear and shake her head in mystification at the strange questions.

"Did unlawful carnal knowledge occur?" asked the prosecutor. (She stared blankly at him.)

"Did he have sexual intercourse with you?" (Still no response.)

"Was there actual penetration?" (She shook her head in bemusement.)

"Did he put his penis in your vagina?"

The witness flung an imploring look at the judge, "I dunno know what 'e means", she cried. The judge leaned over the bench and stared into her face. "Now listen to me, little girl", he said, loudly and clearly, "*Did he fuck you?*".

The witness's relief was obvious, as a smile broke over her face. "Yes, sir, he sure did", she said emphatically.

"Thank you", said the judge. "Now you may proceed, Mr Prosecutor."

WHEN GIVING EVIDENCE, a witness is adjured to remember to be explicit about what was actually said. This exchange occurred in Canberra, during cross-examination of a police witness:

Barrister: I put it to you that this is what he said to you, or words to this effect: "Some bloody idiot ran into me as I was going around the corner". Those were the words he used in the cafe?

Witness: That is incorrect.

Barrister: And that he did not use the words, "This bastard ran me off the fucking road", at all – I am putting to you that he did not use those words?

Witness: He *did* use those words.

Barrister: And he did not say, as you claim he did: "This fucking bastard came around the fucking corner on the left side of the fucking road and ran me into the fucking gutter and into the fucking pole". He did

not use that expression at all, is what I am putting to you?
Witness (after long consideration): From my recollection, I think you have got one too many "fuckings" in there.

HIS HONOUR: He said you called him a pot-bellied old bastard.
Witness: Your Honour, I did not. I would not use such language.
His Honour: What *did* you call him?
Witness: I called him a piggy-eyed, pot-bellied, rotten, filthy animal.

COUNSEL: The point I am making – and the law is explicit and clear on the point – is that it is inadmissable except of sexual activity, and talking about sex is not sexual activity, Your Honour ...
Witness: It is if you have one of those phone calls.

A WELL-KNOWN JUDGE of the District Court asked a housebreaker whether he wanted to advance any reasons as to why he should not be sentenced to prison.
Housebreaker: As the Lord is my judge, I did not do it.
His Honour: He is not; I am; you did.

THIS EFFORT WAS TOPPED by a Brisbane barrister who specialises in Family Law, when he took the witness box in the course of the hearing of his own divorce application.

In blasé fashion he took the oath, then sat back in the witness box with one arm flung nonchalantly over the rail, nodding in affirmation as his counsel rattled off the formal opening questions:

Counsel: Is your full name so-and-so? Do you reside at so-and-so? Are you the husband in these proceedings? Is your wife's full name so-and-so? I show you marriage certificate dated so-and-so. Are you the bridegroom mentioned therein? Is your wife the bride? Do you swear that to the best of your knowledge and belief, the affidavits you have filed in this matter are true and correct?

Witness (speaking as someone who had memorised the script): It is. I do. I am. It is. I am. She is. I do.

———

WITNESSES ARE OFTEN confused by the way our language is used in the courtroom:

Counsel: Now, witness, is your appearance here this morning pursuant to the subpoena forwarded through your solicitors?

Witness: No. This is how I always dress when I go to work.

———

HIS HONOUR: To put it in layman's language for the sake of the jury, the subterranean feet of the homotaxial outcrop encroached into the proposed demarcation line of the channel. That will make it easier for you to understand.

———

WITNESS: In 1979, we found out that my husband had developed terminal cancer, Your Honour.
His Honour: So he is now deceased, is he?
Witness: No, he's dead.

HIS HONOUR: I think it is inexcusable it was not said this clothing had no trace of petrol on it. I hope this practice of not mentioning negatives is not common and will never be repeated.

A VERY STRAIGHT-LACED Supreme Court judge was noted for the double entendres he would drop, quite obliviously.
 Sentencing two men who had pleaded guilty to "carnal knowledge against the order of nature", he said, "It is about time you fellows pulled yourselves together".

PROSECUTING COUNSEL: Your Honour, I believe we can dispose of this witness before lunch.
Defence Counsel: Dispose of him, Your Honour? I didn't think he was *that* bad a witness.

A GUM-CHEWER WAS BROUGHT to heel by a testy judge. The witness had been slouching in the witness box with his hands in his pockets, cheekily chewing gum with his mouth open.
 This so irritated the judge that he slammed his hand down onto the bench and shouted, "Witness, do not masticate in my court!".

"Sorry, Your Honour", said the witness, whipping his hands out of his pockets.

BARRISTER: And what led you to believe the defendant was under the influence of liquor?
Police Witness: Because he was argu – argumen – argumenta – argumenterary – he could not pronounce his words.

HIS HONOUR: Have you anything to say before I impose sentence?
Accused: I cannot read or write.
His Honour: Is that all you have to say?
Accused: I cannot spell, either.

BARRISTER: Have you got any general comments specifically?

HIS HONOUR: When the vehicle came to rest, was it over the centre line or on its correct side of the road?
Witness: Yes.
His Honour: Yes – what?
Witness: Yes, *Sir*, Your Honour.

THE EVIDENCE TURNED ON whether the witness (a new Australian) could read English well enough to understand a document he professed to have read. The prosecutor needed to establish how well he could spell:

THE RIGHT WORD

Prosecutor: Can you spell most English words?
Witness: Of course, I can spell.
Prosecutor: Can you, for instance, spell the word, "duck"?
Witness: That's easy. D-I-K, duck.

THIS STATEMENT FROM the judge elicited a look of consternation from a jury member: "It is for you, the jury, to judge the various weights of the witnesses".

COURT IN THE ACT

SOMETIMES, IN THE SEARCH for clarity, lawyers can become stuck in a mire they did not anticipate:
Counsel: When you say someone is industrious, what does that word mean to you?
Witness: Well, that is when you run around with other women and have sex with other women, and stuff like that.
Counsel: I see. Are you able to read and write?
Witness: Not too good.

QUESTION: Just answer the questions as to the events as they occurred. Do not give us any of your opinions about the accused; is that clear?
Answer: Yes.
Question: Now, just giving us the events as you saw them, and no opinions of your own, would you tell the court when you first saw the accused?
Answer: About 10 am, I looked out of my kitchen window, and I saw the mongrel bastard coming up the drive.

IN A LONG-AGO TRIAL in a far western Queensland town, a defence counsel with a fine sense of theatre and timing was able to turn to dramatic advantage a witness's reluctance to utter a word rarely used in polite society.

The witness, an elderly woman of deep religious convictions, found it impossible to articulate what the victim had once said to her. Eventually, the barrister coaxed her to write it on a piece of paper.

Taking it from her, he made a great show of reading its contents, raising his eyebrows, and shaking his head meaningfully, before folding it neatly and placing it in his pocket. He then went on with another line of questioning.

Thoroughly frustrated, the opposing barrister interrupted: "Well, what was on the paper? Aren't you going to tell us what she said?" he demanded. The defence counsel turned slowly and stared at his opponent. "Get fucked", he said.

A babble of voices rose from the gallery as everyone repeated to each other what the defence counsel had said. The opposing barrister grew red in the face, leapt to his feet, and shouted that the defence counsel be held in contempt. Meanwhile, the defence counsel stood quietly in his place.

Eventually, the judge brought the court back to order. "Please explain yourself, Mr ... ", he ordered.

"Your Honour," replied the defence counsel ingenuously, "I merely told him , 'Get fucked,' which was the answer to the question he asked me. That is what the witness wrote on the piece of paper."

He had achieved his objective. His opponent was thoroughly discomfited for the rest of the day.

EVEN WHEN THE CORRECT and most explicit words are used, some people have difficulty in understanding what is said:

His Honour (to counsel): Your submission is totally irresponsible, in fact, asinine. I find it incomprehensible that you come before me with a submission so utterly spurious, unfounded, and without any case law at all to support it. What you put to me is quite without point, and I find your submission – well, moronic, in fact.

COURT IN THE ACT

Barrister: Am I to infer that Your Honour is not entirely with me at this point?

SHERIFF'S OFFICER *(to jury, when visiting them at one o'clock in the morning, after they had been locked up all night):* Good morning, gentlemen.
Foreman: Eleven gentlemen, actually, and one bastard.

THERE HAVE BEEN MANY FLORID and immoderate speeches made in courtrooms; but special applause must go to a United States judge, sitting in the Federal District Court of the Territory of New Mexico in 1881, in an adobe stable used as a temporary courtroom. He was sentencing a man convicted of a foul murder:

> José Manual Miguel Xavier Gonzales, in a few short weeks it will be spring. The snows of winter will flee away, the ice will vanish, and the air will become soft and balmy. In short, the annual miracle of the years will awaken and come to pass, but you won't be there.
>
> The rivulet will run its soaring course to the sea, the timid desert flowers will put forth their tender shoots, the glorious valley of this imperial domain will blossom as the rose. Still, you won't be there to see.
>
> From every treetop some wild woods songster will carol his mating song, butterflies will sport in the sunshine, the busy bee will hum happily as it pursues its accustomed vocation, the gentle breeze will tease the tassels of the wild grasses and all nature, José Manuel Miguel Xavier Gonzales, will be glad but you.
>
> You won't be here to enjoy it because I command the sheriff or some officers of the county to lead you to some remote spot, swing you by the neck from a

knotting bough of some sturdy oak, and let you hang
until you are dead. After then, José Manuel Miguel
Xavier Gonzales, I further command that such officers
retire quickly from your dangling corpse, that vultures
may descend from the heavens upon your filthy body
until nothing shall remain but the bare, bleached
bones of a cold-blooded, copper-coloured, blood-thirsty,
throat-cutting, chilli-eating, sheep-herding, murdering
son-of-a-bitch.

A FINAL SUBMISSION

Pen writers are disappearing from Australia's Courts and Inquiries. Machines are replacing all those stalwarts who wrote for hours (before computers, back-up tapes and RSI became fashionable) easing their "writer's cramp" during the lunch break by running hot and cold water over their hands, and sustaining each other with friendship and laughter.

With this book, I salute them.

If what I have recorded here seems irreverent, disrespectful, or inane, I simply cite, in my own defence, the following extract from transcript:

BARRISTER: Was there any insanity in your family?
Witness: Well, my father had a nervous breakdown when I was 14 years of age.
Barrister: You do not suggest from that, that he was insane, or had some kind of mental impairment?
Witness: Not from that, no – but, well, he *did* spend 42 years in the Public Service!

... I rest my case.